بسم الله الرحمن الرحيم

In the Name of [illegible]rciful

When Christians Ask; The Quran Answers

When Christians Ask; The Quran Answers

ISBN: 0-9728518-6-0

Library of Congress Catalog Card Number: 2004116818

Manufactured in the United States of America

Multi-National Muslim Committee (MNMC)
PO Box 3491
Newtown CT. 06470

http://www.MuslimPublisher.com

For sales and distribution, contact:
Email: order@MuslimPublisher.com

Publisher's Cataloging in Publication

Mohamed Ghounem
When Christians Ask; The Quran Answers
[Mohamed Ghounem]
1st ed.
p. cm.
Includes bibliographical references and index.
Preassigned LCCN: 2004116818
ISBN: 0-9728518-6-0

1. Quran --Relation to the Bible. I. Title.
2. Islam --Relations --Judaism. II. Title.
3. Islam --Relations –Christianity. III. Title.
4. Apologists.

BP134.G4 2005

Also by Mohamed Ghounem

101 Ways Islam Gives Love to the Bible

101 Bible Quotes on Christ Disproving Trinity

The Apple and the Crucifix: Christianity Revealed

Who is Our Savior? Allah or Jesus

When Jews Ask: The Quran Answers

Leaving Judaism for Islam: Jews Speak Out

Jews and Muslims Agree: From Laws to Love

Why We Die: From Ancient to Modern Philosophies

TABLE OF CONTENTS

TABLE OF CONTENTS

TABLE OF CONTENTS

Introduction

The Bible was once pure, yet over the centuries, scribal, copyist and linguist errors have caused the divine words to be written, copied, and translated wrong. The Quran cures these human insertions that have caused confusion in the Bible. The Quran mends major manipulations that manifest themselves between the scribes of Moses compared to the scribes of Jesus, causing the fault line between Jews and Christians. Where the Bible makes erroneous single assertions, the Quran counters these contradictions with accurate detailed descriptions. Where the Bible lists multiple conflicting exegeses, the Quran helps the Bible with a single powerful compendium.

About this book:

This research study is essentially four books in one:

1) A book of **Questions;** listing over 100 questions that arise from reading the Bible.
2) A book of **Excuses;** listing attempts by the top Biblical apologists to remedy the errancies
3) A book of **Replies;** listing refutations to the excuses by Biblicists, so that the reader can make an objective comparison.
4) A book of **Answers;** listing the miraculous ways the Quran accomplishes what millenniums of Bible scholars could not. In this comprehensive analysis, you will find how the Quran gives clear and concise answers for Christians.

Overall, this is a book of unity, settling the differences between Jews and Christians:

"And We sent down the Book (Quran) to thee for the express purpose, that thou shouldst make clear to them those things in which they differ, and that it should be a guide and a mercy to those who believe." (Quran 16:64)

The Purpose:

The purpose of this book is multidimensional:

To present harmony to the children of Abraham. Through agreement comes love, and love is the opposite of war. Peaceful tranquility is the effect of the Quran on warring families, neighbors, tribes, countries and religions. The Quran unites over a billion humans from all ethnic and socioeconomic backgrounds, together shoulder to shoulder and foot to foot, in worship to One Creator.

To solidify what many Muslims have been stating, that the Quran came to help the Bible. The Quran is the Divine arbitrator of the Bible, judging between Jews and Christians and being the unifier of the two.

To clarify an often overlooked miracle in the Quran; There are almost a million words in the entire Bible, hence it's splendidly incredible and absolutely impossible to filter through these thousands of words and identify and correct words that were not known to be wrong until centuries later. The Quran, coming from the Lord of the heavens and the earth, is able to do this divine task for humans to bear witness.

To dispel myths that the Quran copied the Bible. Demonstrating that the Quran is not the copy, it is the answer.

Another myth is that the Quran is from ungodly sources. As we will witness, the Quran answers Bible issues on topics of *morality, fairness, and equality* to name a few. God wants us to be moral, just, and equitable, hence the Quran is from God.

Common Christian excuses and their Reply:

In recognition of the disagreements within the Bible, apologists have tried to give answers for the discrepant and abnormal passages within the Bible.

In the principal of fairness, we are providing the reader with the opportunity to objectively analyze studious answers by top Biblicists, along with diagnostic Islamic replies to their rationale.

The reply section we have provided also proves that the recent field of Biblical apologists is insufficient compared to the corrections God revealed in the Quran almost 1,400 years ago.

Included in this monumental expedition, is a reply chart that we will be frequently referring to, in reply to the answers we present from Biblical apologists.

The Reply Chart

Answer A: The irrational can be rational at a later time. *When scientists find irrational discoveries, they continue to research the item because a rational explanation may be found at a later time.*
(Reply A)- In principle, this is a valid point, but it has been over 2,000 Years since a Prophet from the Bible has appeared or reappeared. Hence, God has sent the Holy Quran to explain the anomalies in the Bible. God blessed humans with the tools to succeed in this life for this life and the hereafter. What is unexplained in the Bible must be explained. This explanation comes from the Qur'an, the final revelation. When people assume that the unexplainable will never be explained or explained at a later time, then people must look to the Quran for immediate clarification and a fulfillment of the void.
Answer B: Humans cannot fully understand the Revelation of God, unless the spirit of God is with us. *Because humans are imperfect, we cannot perfectly interpret what God says.*
(Reply B)- This is a circular argument based on (1 Corinthians 2:14) "the natural man receiveth not the things of the Spirit of God for they are foolishness to him; neither can he know them for they are spiritually discerned." This has led us to the conclusion that one would need to be in a certain spiritually altered state of mind, a self-hypnosis that the Bible is true. It is unacceptable that one has to be in a mental stupor to accept the Bible. When the mind is clear of internal or external intoxicants, only then can we judge clearly between the Truth and distortion. (1 Corinthians 14:33) "For God is not the author of confusion"
Answer C: You must understand the context of the verse.
(Reply C)- This is a false claim because there are an abundant amount of chapters in the Bible that contain no context, for example; Proverbs. The verses are a number of independent statements that skip through different subjects. Other examples include the discrepancies between Samuel, Kings, and Chronicles which contain verses about people and numbers which invalidate the out of context argument. Context is important but will not be automatically sanctioned if an attempt to use that excuse is made.
Answer D: A vital word is difficult to interpret because it's rarely used in the Bible
(Reply D)- Everything in Scripture is important for human beings. Our guidance from Allah comes from scripture. Furthermore, The Quran was given to us to clear the obscurity that is found within the Bible.
Answer E; That's what it says but that's not what it means
(Reply E)- If the Bible writers meant something else, then why didn't they record it as

it was meant? Were their pens prevented from writing what the scribes meant? Those who use this answer claim they know Greek and Hebrew better than the ancient Greek and Hebrew writers in Biblical times. The Bible translators utilize a vast amount of vocabulary dictionaries and ancient texts to pick the exact interpretation. In turn, the process itself of choosing Biblical words, invalidate their answer.

Answer F: Copyist Error

(Reply F)- Again, Bible apologists want us to believe the Bible is 100% inerrant when they themselves admit that the transmitters also made copying errors. This is another unacceptable answer because it is admitting the Bible we have today has human errors, hence not a divine book. The answer that the Bible is all human and all divine is unacceptable just as the fallacy that Jesus is all human and all divine.

For example, an item is either made in China or made in the USA, it can not be made in both places, unless it's transported between the two, at that point, it's no longer 100% Chinese or all American, it's diluted and hence no longer 100% authentic. The Quran corrects this type of error by stating "We made the Quran easy to remember". Millions of Muslims, since the Angel Gabriel recited the Holy Quran to Prophet Muhammad (pbuh), have memorized the entire Quran, so that not a syllable has changed within the Quran in over 1400 years, in comparison to the Bible which has been copied and rewritten many times over the years.

Answer G; Later Scripture replaces Previous Scripture.

(Reply G)- If this is true, then over a billion Muslims state that the Quran, which came after the Bible, supersedes past revelations (Torah and Gospel). The fact is, God promised to Abraham that the covenant of Laws is forever and everlasting, as well as Jesus himself declaring he did not come to change the laws; "Do not think that I came to destroy the Law or the Prophets. I did not come to destroy but to fulfill. For verily I say unto you, Till heaven and earth pass, one jot or one title shall in no wise pass from the law, till all be fulfilled. " (Matthew 5:17-18).

Answer H; Existing Biblical words are being taken literally instead of symbolically or metaphorically.

(Reply H)- Apologists try to fall back on this answer when common sense fails. An entire sentence is claimed to be literal except for the divergent word in the sentence, at which that one errant word is categorized as "metaphorical" See (Genesis 5:5) for example. We cannot selectively choose which words in a sentence or scenario are figurative while the surrounding words in the sentence and chapter are literal.

Answer I; Translation error

(Reply I)- Apologists admit that some of the errors in the Bible are attributed to translation errors from Hebrew to Greek to German to English. Of course, any linguist would also admit that no word could be perfectly translated from one language to another, especially from one language funneled down through four languages.

This may be acceptable in earthly texts, but this answer is unacceptable in Divine Scripture, especially in the light of the Quran. This answer is corrected by the Quran because the Quran is only accepted as authentic in its original language (Arabic). Yet, Bible apologists want us to still believe that the Bible is Divine and inerrant in every language of the world, and at the same time confess that there are translation errors in the Bible, when that is linguistically impossible.

The Bible lacks the linguistic pillar of support because the Aramaic language is extinct. Furthermore, Christians already accept the Bible in all languages as divine, so if you approached any Christian and told them that only the Aramaic Bible is 100% divine, they would call you a heretic. The Quran simply fulfils what the Bible lacks: a stable means of communication.

Immediately we see a serious disadvantage for the Bible, because no book can be perfectly translated. Therefore God blessed the Bible followers by sending another original "Reading" (Quran in Arabic) since the original Bible has been lost in translation after translation, so the Bible followers no longer had to hang their eternal salvation on one of the hundreds of mistranslated Bible words. Monotheists now have a defense against skeptics, they can validly point to word translations, while Bible followers are void of this defense because their English Bibles are considered the exact words of God.

Some Christians assume that the **Greek** manuscripts of the Gospel is the original language**,** although the prevailing consensus is that Jesus **spoke** Aramaic, therefore, any language **other** than Aramaic (Greek, German, English), is a **translation** of the **Aramaic**. The assumed original Gospel is actually a **translation** from the verbal Aramaic into the scribbled Greek. Thus there is no way for Christians to use the **translation excuse** because there is no way to verify the errors made between what Jesus said **verbally** in **Aramaic** (there is no audio recordings of his words) compared to the Greek **translation** of his speeches. There would be obviously many errors because the Greeks were predominantly **idol worshippers** in those days, opposite of the Semitic speaking Jews.

(1.) Questions on the Old Testament **(A.) God**

Omniscient & Omnipotent, Creator and Knower of Everything including our thoughts!

God can be seen?

Jewish Vs. Christian Question; There is a discrepancy in the Bible about whether God has been seen or not. The Christians, based on the assumption that Jesus is God, claim we have seen God, in flesh form.

Furthermore, the Bible lists some Prophets who have seen God before Jesus came to earth; "And I will take away my hand, and thou shalt see my back parts." (Exodus 33:23)

"And the Lord spoke to Moses face to face, as a man speaketh to his friend." (Exodus 33:11)

"For I have seen God face to face, and my life is preserved." (Genesis 32:30)
Vs No one has ever seen God (Exodus 33:17, 20, John 1:18, 1 Timothy 6:15-16)

Priest's Excuse; People were seeing visions, or dreams, or the Angel of the Lord (Numbers 22:22-26; Judges 13:1-21) and not really God Himself.

Muslim Reply: Those cited passages do not say 'vision, dream, or Angel' of the Lord, they say that people saw God (Exodus 24:9-11), that God was seen, and that He appeared as God (Exodus 6:2-3).

Quranic Answer: Some Christians claim they need to see Jesus (in graven images such as crosses, paintings, and statues), to believe and or to remember God exists. In response to this, all of nature is proof that God exists.

Furthermore, how can we withstand the magnificent sight of our God who created the Sun and all the other stars in the Universe? The Lord of the heavens and the earth is too brilliant for our eyes to view Him in this life. Even Prophets have not been able to see Him as God says to Moses in this verse:

"When Moses came at Our appointed time and his Lord spoke to him, he said: My Lord! show me (Thyself), so that I may look upon Thee. He said: You cannot (bear to) see Me but look at the mountain, if it remains firm in its place, then will you see Me; but when his Lord manifested His glory to the mountain He made it crumble and Moses fell down in a swoon; then when he recovered, he said: Glory be to Thee, I turn to Thee, and I am the first of the believers." (Quran 7:143)

God is Exalted from those who make pictures and idols stating that it is God, when they are falsely describing He who we cannot see:

"Glorified be the Lord of the heavens and the earth, the Lord of the Throne! Exalted is He from all that they ascribe (to Him)." (Quran 43:82)

"Verily! Those who fear their Lord unseen, theirs will be forgiveness and a great reward" (Quran 67:12)

We now understand that our human sensors are not capable of getting even a glimpse of the Originator of the Universe.

Destroying the World Again?

Jewish Vs. Christian Question; "…I will not again curse the ground any more for man's sake; for the imagination of man's heart is evil from his youth; neither will I again smite any more every thing living, as I have done." (Genesis 8:21) *Vs* "the heavens will pass away with a great noise, and the elements will melt with fervent heat; both the earth and the works that are in it will be burned up" (2 Peter 3:10).

Priest's Excuse; Biblical apologists grasp at straws by claiming what God meant was that the same flood method would not be used again; "as I have done."

Muslim Reply: What the passage actually reads is "neither will I again smite any more every thing living, as I have done" not as I have done with water or I will smite everything living in a different way next time. In a logical interpretation without making false insertions, this passage says, "I killed all before and I won't do it again". "as I have done" is a confession, not an omission of genocide tactics for the presumed next time.

Quranic Answer: First, there has never yet been destruction to all people according to the Quran. God does not destroy innocent people and will save those whom He will. The option is open for God to destroy the sinners;

"Seest thou not that Allah created the heavens and the earth in Truth? If He so will, He can remove you and put (in your place) a new Creation?" (Quran 14:19)

Therefore, God in the Quran does not make any contradictory promises as in the Bible. The Quran displays an open option that shows a just God whom will do as He wills.

(B.) Science

Shape of Earth

Jewish Vs. Christian Question; Despite the 180-Degree shift by modern Biblical apologists in comparison to the previous 15 centuries of Christian scholars, we are still left with passages in the Bible, which strongly indicate the earth is flat;

"And he shall set up an ensign for the nations, and shall assemble the outcasts of Israel, and gather together the dispersed of Judah from the four corners of the earth" (Isaiah 11:12)

"that it might take the earth by the edges and shake the wicked out of it" (Job 38:13)"

"And after these things I saw four angels standing on four corners of the earth, holding the four winds of the earth, that the wind should not blow on the earth, nor on the sea, nor on any tree." (Revelation 7:1)

"The tree grew, and was strong, and the height thereof reached unto heaven, and the sight thereof to the ends of all the earth" (Daniel 4:11)

"Again, the devil taketh him up into an exceeding high mountain, and showeth him all the kingdoms of the world, and the glory of them" (Matthew 4:8)

These passages clearly indicated that the earth has four corners and that the entire earth could be seen from one end to the other. Modern day Bible followers may not interpret those passages as such, but centuries of Christian scholars beforehand did just that. The centuries of Christian scholars who support the flat earth belief are;

Lactantius (AD 245–325), a professional rhetorician who converted to Christianity mid-life. Severian of Gabala (380). Cosmas Indicopleustes, sixth century Eastern Greek Christian who claimed the Earth was flat and lay beneath the heavens (consisting of a rectangular vaulted arch). In the books, "Tremendous Treks" by Peter Kent and "Christopher Columbus" by Lucio Sorre, the popular Christian theory of the earth being flat are well documented amongst the masses.

Priest's Excuse; That's what is says but that's not what it means, the four corners are actually references to north, south, east and west.

Muslim Reply: It is unacceptable to claim that the four corners were referring to navigational directions for three obvious reasons. The first is that when the Bible depicts navigational directions, then it actually says those directions and not the square description of "four corners of the earth."

"And thy seed shall be as the dust of the earth, and thou shalt spread abroad to the west, and to the east, and to the north, and to the south: and in thee and in thy seed shall all the families of the earth be blessed." (Genesis 28:14)

The second reason why the apologists attempt to change the meaning of "four corners" fails is that the term "four corners" is used elsewhere to mean a square structure;

"And, behold, there came a great wind from the wilderness, and smote the four corners of the house, and it fell upon the young men, and they are dead; and I only am escaped alone to tell thee." (Job 1:19)

The third reason is that the Bible writers state that they can see all four corners of the earth;

"And after these things I saw four angels standing on the four corners of the earth" (Revelation 7:1)

Hence, confirming the earth is flat because if you can see all four corners of your house, then you are standing on a flat ground.

Quranic Answer: The Quran clearly and consistently states the shape of the earth is spherical: "…and the earth, after that, He (God) made it 'dahaha' (oval shape)" (Quran 79:30)

On Earth Forever?

Jewish Vs. Christian Question; The earth will last forever (Ecclesiastes 1:4) *Vs* The earth will be destroyed (2 Peter 3:10)

Priest's Excuse; Mistranslation.

Muslim Reply: If the Bible mistranslates a word as grand as the earth, then how can we trust anything the Bible says about matters as small as humans?

Quranic Answer: The life of this world is short if we all but knew how short;

"On the day when the earth will be changed to other than the earth, and the heavens (also will be changed) and they (humans) will come forth unto Allah, the One, the Almighty" (Quran 14:48)

(C.) LAWS

Covet Gifts?

Jewish Vs. Christian Question; Do not covet worldly material (Exodus 20:17) *Vs* Covet worldly material. (1 Corinthians 12:31)

Priest's Excuse; That is what it says but that is not what it means. In (1 Corinthians 12:31), covet means desire lawfully.

Muslim Reply: Any envy is evil in the Bible (Proverbs 14:30). Secondly, (Exodus 20:17) does not differentiate between lawful or unlawful coveting. Lastly, worldly temptation in the Bible only comes from the devil, thus always unlawful;

"Let no one say when he is tempted, "I am being tempted by God"; for God cannot be tempted by evil, and He Himself does not tempt anyone. But each one is tempted when he is carried away and enticed by his own lust." (James 1:13-14)

Quranic Answer: The Quran corrects the Bible by consistently specifying that coveting is a sin:

"And covet not the thing in which Allah hath made some of you excel others. Unto men a fortune from that which they have earned, and unto women a fortune from that which they have earned. (Envy not one another) but ask Allah of His bounty. Lo! Allah is ever Knower of all things." (Quran 4:32)

Celibacy Preferred?

Jewish Vs. Christian Question; Marriage encouraged (Genesis 2:18-24, 1 Timothy 4:1- 5) Vs Marriage discouraged (1 Corinthians 7:8)

Priest's Excuse; That is what it says but that is not what it means. Paul is not saying, "don't get married"; he is merely stating, "it's better not to be married."

Muslim Reply: First, this adds to the contradiction because the Bible says it is better to be married; "Then the Lord God said, "It is not good for the man to live alone. I will make a suitable companion to help him." (Genesis 2:18)

Secondly, further down in (1st Corinthians), Paul reiterates himself by telling the single people not to get married; "Are you unmarried? Then don't look for a wife." (1 Corinthians 7:27)

This commandment by Paul in the Bible has been followed to the letter by Christian Priests worldwide, forsaking marriage for a life of celibacy. This proves that Paul is not merely making a suggestion, but instead creating a conflicting law.

Quranic Answer: Islam agrees with human nature. Islam is well known as the "natural religion" for Islam is in harmony with a human's body, mind, and soul. The Quran teaches us to mary as it is our nature to have a companion:

"Marry those among you who are single, or the virtuous ones among yourselves, male or female: if they are in poverty, Allah will give them means out of His grace: for Allah encompasseth all, and He knoweth all things." (Quran 24:32)

"This day are (all) things good and pure made lawful unto you. The food of the People of the Book is lawful unto you and yours is lawful unto them. Lawful unto you in marriage are (not only) chaste women who are believers, but chaste women among the People of the Book, revealed before your time, - when ye give them their due dowers, and desire chastity, not lewdness, nor secret intrigues if any one rejects faith, fruitless is his work, and in the Hereafter he will be in the ranks of those who have lost (all spiritual good)." (Quran 5:5)

In conclusion, the hierarchies in the Christian religion such as Priests and Nuns who do not marry, are in violation of nature. While all Muslims including Sheikhs, Imams, Muftis, and Ministers are encouraged to marry. Islam agrees with how Allah fashioned us.

Work on the Sabbath?

Jewish Vs. Christian Question; Do not work on the Sabbath (Exodus 31:15) *Vs* Prophet Jesus worked on the Sabbath (John 5:16, Matthew 12:1-3, 5)

Priest's Excuse; Jesus was God, thus he was allowed to break the Sabbath

Muslim Reply: Jesus declared that God never stops working, even on the Sabbath day (John 5:16) which is correctly confirmed in the (Quran 2:255).

Quranic Answer: The Holy Quran, as a completion of the Bible explains that Jesus was emphasizing the point that the Sabbath was about remembrance, not work. Not working on Sabbath was a judgment placed on rebellious Israelites who considered the new law a curse, because God never rests, the financial restraint put on the Israelites was instead a punishment as perceived in the Bible;

"When will the new moon be gone, that we may sell corn? and the Sabbath, that we may set forth wheat, making the ephah small, and the shekel great, and falsifying the balances by deceit? That we may buy the poor for silver, and the needy for a pair of shoes; yea, and sell the refuse of the wheat?" (Amos 8:4-6)

"Men of Tyre also, who lived in the city, brought in fish and all kinds of wares and sold them on the Sabbath to the people of Judah, and in Jerusalem." (Nehemiah 13:16)

The Sabbath that was issued to the rebellious Hebrews with Moses became an unbearable restraint towards the Bounties of God to the Israelites, then starting with Jesus as a righteous messenger of God and completed with God's reiteration in the Holy Quran, the obedient were forgiven.

Thus, the Holy Quran explains that the Sabbath is a day of remembrance, rather than rest. The merciful removal of the restriction from God's bounty is specified in the following verses:

"O ye who believe! When the call is proclaimed to prayer on Friday (the Day of Assembly), hasten earnestly to the Remembrance of Allah, and leave off business (and traffic): That is best for you if ye but knew! "And when the Prayer is finished, then may ye disperse through the land, and seek of the Bounty of Allah: and celebrate the Praises of Allah often (and without stint): that ye may prosper." "(Quran 62:9-10)

Good Laws?

Jewish Vs. Christian Question; The Laws are delightful (Psalms 119:35) Vs The Laws are a curse (Galatians 3:10-13)

Priest's Excuse; The laws were good to follow until the resurrection. After the resurrection, the laws were done away with; "Purge out therefore the old leaven, that ye may be a new lump, as ye are unleavened. For even Christ our Passover is sacrificed for us" (1 Corinthians 5:7)

Muslim Reply: It is a faulty notion to claim the laws, which were followed for millenniums, were only made to be temporary. Both the God of Abraham and Jesus state the laws are forever;

"Everlasting" ,"For All Generations", "a Perpetual Ordinance " (Exodus 27:21; 28:43; 29:28; 30:21; 31:17; Leviticus 6:18, 22; 7:34, 36; 10:9, 15; 17:7; 23:14, 21, 41; 24:3; Numbers 10:8; 15:15; 18:8, 11, 19, 23; 19:10; Deuteronomy 5:29; Psalms 119:160) and is Not to be changed or taken away from (Deuteronomy 4:2; 12:32).

Jesus confirms the Laws are for all generations and everlasting by following the laws (Matthew 8:4, 26:19, John 7:10). Actions speak louder than words and besides the actions of Jesus keeping the Everlasting Laws, Jesus also states;

"Think not that I am come to destroy the law, or the prophets: I am not come to destroy, but to fulfill. For verily I say unto you, Till heaven and earth pass, one jot or one title shall in no wise pass from the law, till all be fulfilled." (Matthew 5:17-18)

In conclusion, the God of Abraham, the Prophets, and the Messiah all say the Laws are unending. The Righteous have one Enemy, he who leads people astray through lethargy.

Quranic Answer: God, through the Holy Quran explains that it is a combination of Faith and Works that gives us Salvation:

"For Him (alone) is prayer in Truth: any others that they call upon besides Him hear them no more than if they were to stretch forth their hands for water to reach their mouths but it reaches them not: for the prayer of those without Faith is nothing but (futile) wandering (in the mind)." (Quran 13:14)

The Holy Quran explains that works are to our benefit:

"O you whose hearts have been touched with the divine hand: When you intend to stand before God for performing your act of worship, then ablution becomes a duty. Wash your faces, your hands and the forearms up to the elbows, and with your wet hands wipe your heads, then wash your feet to the ankles....- God does not intend to put you in difficulty but only to make you sound headed men of proper discipline and excellent mind, and to set you upon a course of purity of thought and action, for the actions of men are best interpreters of their thoughts, and He means to make all grace abound in you that you may hopefully actuate yourselves with the feeling of gratitude and gratefulness and lift Him your inward sight." (Quran 5:6)

The Holy Quran teaches us that Jesus only came to clarify the previous scripture, not to change it, and he came to promote the most important law, to worship our Creator:

"When Jesus came with clear proofs (of Allah's Sovereignty), he said: I have come unto you with wisdom, and to make plain some of that concerning which ye differ. So keep your duty to Allah, and obey me."

"For Allah, He is my Lord and your Lord: so worship ye Him: this is a Straight Way." (Quran 43:63-64)

Poor or Preachers?

Jewish Vs. Christian Question; There is some discord in the Bible regarding who is to receive tithes;

When a rich man asked Jesus, Jesus replied; "If thou wilt be perfect, go and sell that thou hast, and -give to the poor-, and thou shalt have treasure in heaven" (Matthew 19:21)

Also;

"At the end of every third year you shall bring out all the tithe of your produce in that year, and shall deposit it in your town. And the Levite, because he has no portion or inheritance among you, and the alien, the orphan and the widow who are in your town, shall come and eat and be satisfied, in order that the Lord your God may bless you in all the work of your hand which you do (Deuteronomy 14:28-29).

Tithes went to the poor, the widows, and the orphans. Yet, In the Gospel, Paul claims that he should take the tithes;

"In the same way the Lord has given orders that those who preach the Gospel should be supported by those who accept it." (1 Corinthians 9:14)

This is a false claim by Paul, for nowhere in the Bible does Jesus or God command to give money to those who preach the Gospel, though unfortunately it seems that the Church follows Paul more than God.

Priest's Excuse; Paul was saying he would take the money to redistribute it to the poor.

Muslim Reply: Paul is clearly saying that those who preach should get paid for it. Furthermore, Jesus never said, "give me the money to redistribute it to the poor." Instead, Jesus taught people to give directly to the poor as Muslims do.

Quranic Answer: Islam corrects these man-inserted laws in the Bible;

"(Charity is) for those in need, who, in Allah's cause are restricted (from travel), and cannot move about in the land, seeking (For trade or work): the ignorant man thinks, because of their modesty, that they are free from want. Thou shalt know them by their (Unfailing) mark: They beg not importunately from all the sundry. And whatever of good ye give, be assured Allah knoweth it well." (Quran 2:273)

"They give food, out of love for Him (Allah), to the poor, the orphan, and the slave, saying: We feed you only for Allah's pleasure - we desire from you neither reward nor thanks." (Quran 76:8-9)

The difference between the Church and Islamic charity is that large amounts of money are left with individuals in the Church, therefore opening the opportunity for corruption, while in Islam, most of the charity goes directly to the poor.

To Fast?

Jewish Vs. Christian Question; Fasting is for three weeks (Daniel 10:2-3) *Vs* Fasting is for forty days (Deuteronomy 9:9-18, Matthew 4:1-2)

There is no consistent standard or time frame taught in the Bible. It is obvious that many of the Prophets in the Bible fasted, hence we must "be like them" but no clear guidance is within the Bible as to how long to fast.

Priest's Excuse; None available.

Quranic Answer: Unlike the Bible, the Holy Quran specifies the period for fasting as being one month:

"Ramadan is the (month) in which was sent down the Quran, as a guide to mankind, also clear (Signs) for guidance and judgment (Between right and wrong). So every one of you who is present (at his home) during that month should spend it in fasting, but if any one is ill, or on a journey, the prescribed period (Should be made up) by days later. Allah intends every facility for you; He does not want to put to difficulties. (He wants you) to complete the prescribed period, and to glorify Him in that He has guided you; and perchance ye shall be grateful." (Quran 2:185)

Thus, the Holy Quran clarifies the standard date, time, reason, and method of fasting, unlike the Bible.

The Fate of apostates?

Jewish Vs. Christian Question; Does the Bible claim that if someone turns away from God, they are lost forever and to be killed;

"For how can those who abandon their faith be brought back to repent again? They were once in God's light; they tasted heaven's gift and received their share of the Holy Spirit; they knew from experience that God's word is good, and they had felt the powers of the coming age. And then they abandoned their faith! It is impossible to bring them back to repent again, because they are again crucifying the Son of God and exposing him to public shame." (Hebrews 6:4-6)

And

"But when the righteous turneth away from his righteousness, and committeth iniquity, and doeth according to all the abominations that the wicked man doeth, shall he live? All his righteousness that he hath done shall not be mentioned: in his trespass that he hath trespassed, and in his sin that he hath sinned, in them shall he die." (Ezekiel 18:24)

Priest's Excuse; Later Scripture overrules previous scriptures

Muslim Reply: Here the Biblicists ignore that the superseding scripture in the Bible also confirms apostates are to be put to death;

"If we decide to go on sinning after we have learned the truth, there is no longer any sacrifice for sins. There is nothing but fear in waiting for the judgment and the terrible fire that will destroy all those who live against God. Anyone who refused to obey the law of Moses was found guilty from the proof given by two or three witnesses. He was put to death without mercy. So what do you think should be done to those who do not respect the Son of God, who look at the blood of the agreement that made them holy as no different from others' blood, who insult the Spirit of God's grace? Surely they should have a much worse punishment." (Hebrews 10:26-29)

Quranic Answer: Our Merciful Lord shows benevolence towards those who stray in error, giving the apostate more than one chance to repent. The Quran does not discard human lives ruthlessly as the Bible appears to:

"Those who believe, then reject faith, then believe (again) and (again) reject faith, and go on increasing in unbelief,- Allah will not forgive them nor guide them nor guide them on the way." (Quran 4:137)

Furthermore, in the Holy Quran, the death given to apostates is a spiritual one, for the rejecters of faith lose guidance:

"That is because they believed, then they rejected Faith: So a seal was set on their hearts: therefore they understand not." (Quran 63:3)

Unlike the Bible, the Quran teaches not to physically harm those who do not physically harm us:

"Let there be no compulsion in religion: Truth stands out clear from Error: whoever rejects evil and believes in Allah hath grasped the most trustworthy hand-hold that never breaks. And Allah heareth and knoweth all things." (Quran 2:256)

(D.) History

Adam's Reconciliation?

Jewish Vs. Christian Question; According to the Bible, Adam was not forgiven throughout his entire lifetime for eating from the forbidden tree. Is Adam portrayed in the Bible as a non-repenting sinner throughout his entire life. Because Adam disobeyed God, Adam and all men and women after Adam were cursed and ejected from paradise. We see that even after Jesus came and left the world, Paul still speaks of the accursed Adam;

"Wherefore, as by one man [Adam] sin entered into the world, and death by sin; and so death passed upon all men, for that all have sinned" (Romans 5:12, 14, 1 Corinthians 15:21-22,)

Furthermore, the Bible has no record of Adam repenting, ludicrously though; the Bible says God repented for making Adam (Genesis 6:6) Thus, the Bible backwardly claims that it was God who repented rather than the one who disobeyed Him, Adam.

Priest's Excuse; None available.

Quranic Answer: The Holy Quran corrects the regressive passages that are found within the Bible, clarifying that it was Adam, not God who repented. Hence, God provides the missing reconciliation that granted Adam and his descendants to have an ongoing communication with God:

"Then Adam received from his Lord words (of revelation), and He relented toward him. Lo! He is the Relenting the Merciful. We said: Go down, all of you, from hence; but verily there cometh unto you from Me a guidance; and whoso followeth My guidance, there shall no fear come upon them neither shall they grieve." (Quran 2:37-38)

First to Ascend?

Jewish Vs. Christian Question; No one has ascended into heaven before Jesus (John 3:13) *Vs* Elijah ascended into heaven (2 Kings 2:11)

Priest's Excuse; That is what it says but that is not what it means. Jesus means that no one went to heaven and returned with a message before him.

Muslim Reply: This is an insertion by apologists with no basis in context or meaning of the passage. Besides this excuse being unfounded, it's also incorrect because Elijah is shown within the Bible to have ascended to Heaven and did indeed return with a message before Jesus;

"But I say to you that Elijah has come already, and they did not know him but did to him whatever they wished. Likewise the Son of Man is also about to suffer at their hands." (Matthew 17:12)

Quranic Answer: Unlike the conflicting Bible, the Noble Quran confirms that others before Jesus have ascended into Heaven;

"And (the Jinn who had listened to the Quran said): We had sought the heaven but had found it filled with strong warders and meteors." (Quran 72:8)

Abraham's Father?

Jewish Vs. Christian Question; Does the Bible contain conflicts surrounding Abraham's Father?

In (Genesis 11:26), Abraham's Father is called "Terah", yet in (Luke 3:34), Abraham's Father is called "Thara"

Also, in various Talmudic stories (Midr. Rabbah on Gen. par. 17), Abraham's father is called "Zarah", while Eusebius Pamphili (the ecclesiastical) gives his name as Athar.

Priest's Excuse; Translation error

Muslim Reply: All translation errors are grave errors, but name mistranslations are especially bad because they completely confuse one person for another, similar to the confusion in the Bible as to whether Christ was to be called Jesus or Emanuel.

Quranic Answer: The Quran corrects all the skepticism surrounding the identity of Abraham's father by naming him "Azar" (Quran 6:74), similar to the Greek name Athar as used by Biblical scholars. The Quran stands firm on the identity of Abraham's father and does not present paradoxes pertaining to his name, age, and progeny.

Abraham's Sacrifice?

Jewish Vs. Christian Question; Who was the sacrificial son of Abraham? The Bible claims Isaac was the son to be sacrificed, yet logically and mathematically, the son was Ishmael. The covenant was first made with Abraham and Ishmael;

"This [is] my covenant, which ye shall keep, between me and you and thy seed after thee; Every man child among you shall be circumcised." (Genesis 17:10)

"He that is born in thy house, and he that is bought with thy money, must be circumcised: and my covenant shall be in your flesh for an everlasting covenant." (Genesis 17:13)

The arithmetic of Abraham's age reveals that Ishmael was the son to be sacrificed;

"and Abram [is] a son of eighty and six years in Hagar's bearing Ishmael to Abram." (Genesis 16:16)

"Abraham was ninety-nine years old when he was circumcised in the flesh of his foreskin." (Genesis 17:24)

That makes Abraham's son Ishmael 13, how old is Isaac at this time?

"Abraham was a hundred years old when his son Isaac was born to him." (Genesis 21:5)

That means during the prepared sacrifice, Abraham's only "begotten" son is Ishmael and not Isaac as the Bible conflictingly says (Hebrews 11:17)

Therefore, we see that Isaac was not the only son, in fact, Isaac was not even born yet, and Abraham's only begotten son was Ishmael.

Furthermore, we know that Ishmael has and will be a legitimate son, despite what some Bible commentator's claim;

(Genesis 16:3) "And Sarai Abram's wife took Hagar her maid the Egyptian, after Abram had dwelt ten years in the land of Canaan, and gave her to her husband Abram to be his wife."

(Genesis 25:9) "Then his sons Isaac and Ishmael buried him (Abraham) in the cave of Machpelah, in the field of Ephron the son of Zohar the Hittite, facing Mamre,"

(Genesis 25:12) "Now these are the records of the generations of Ishmael, Abraham's son, whom Hagar the Egyptian, Sarah's maid, bore to Abraham;"

Priest's Excuse; Due to the mother of Ishmael being a bonds woman, Ishmael was not a legitimate son.

Muslim Reply: This excuse is discredited by the passage;

"And Sarah Abram's wife took Hagar her maid the Egyptian, after Abram had dwelt ten years in the land of Canaan, and gave her to her husband Abram to be his wife." (Genesis 16:3)

Therefore, unless the Biblicists are claiming Abraham committed adultery; Hagar was a legitimate wife of Abraham and consequently, Ishmael was a legitimate son of Abraham. Further proof is;

"Then his sons Isaac and Ishmael buried him (Abraham) in the cave of Machpelah, in the field of Ephron the son of Zohar the Hittite, facing Mamre," (Genesis 25:9)

Here, the Bible directly calls Ishmael a son (not stepson or half son) of Abraham, standing equally in front of the grave with Isaac. Although, at one point Abraham and Hagar were separated, that does not invalidate the child Hagar had with Abraham. For example, if two parents get a divorce, the father and son lineage is not broken and the son is still the child of the father.

Quranic Answer: These mistaken identities and miscalculations in the Bible are amended by the Quran listing the correct chronological order;

(Quran 37:99) He said: "I will go to my Lord! He will surely guide me!
(Quran 37:100) "O my Lord! Grant me a righteous (son)!"
(Quran 37:101) So We gave him the good news of a forbearing son.
(Quran 37:102) Then, when (the son) reached (the age of) (serious) work with him, he said: "O my son! I have seen in a vision that I offer thee in sacrifice: now see what is thy view!" (The son) said: "O my father! Do as thou art commanded: thou will find me, if Allah so wills, one of the steadfast!"
(Quran 37:103) So when they had both submitted (to Allah), and he had laid him prostrate on his forehead (for sacrifice),
(Quran 37:104) We called out to him "O Abraham! ...
(Quran 37:105) "Thou hast already fulfilled the vision!" - thus indeed do We reward those who do right.
(Quran 37:106) For this was a clear trial-
(Quran 37:107) And We ransomed him with a momentous sacrifice:
(Quran 37:108) And We left for him among generations (to come) in later times:
(Quran 37:109) "Peace and salutation to Abraham!"
(Quran 37:110) Thus indeed do We reward those who do right.
(Quran 37:111) For he was one of Our believing Servants.
(Quran 37:112) And We gave him the good news of Isaac - a prophet, - one of the Righteous.

Thus, the Quran shows the correct sequential order; Ishmael being born, the sacrifice to be taken place, and then Isaac being born.

Feared Pharaoh?

Jewish Vs. Christian Question; Moses feared Pharaoh (Exodus 2:14-15) *Vs* Moses did not fear Pharaoh (Hebrews 11:27)

Priest's Excuse; None available.

Quranic Answer: Moses was a righteous messenger sent by God to face the evil magic of Pharaoh. After being inspired by God, Moses did not fear Pharaoh or he would have never boldly gone to him. Instead of being a fearful cowardice as wrongfully revealed in the Bible, Moses' true nature of being a source of comfort and security for the people of Israel is displayed. The Quran clarifies the scenario:

"So I fled from you (all) when I feared you; but my Lord has (since) invested me with judgment (and wisdom) and appointed me as one of the messengers." (Quran 26:21)

The Holy Quran consistently fills in the missing puzzle piece to correct the Bible and help clear the confusion of Christians worldwide.

"And We inspired Moses (saying): Throw thy staff! And lo! it swallowed up their lying show." (Quran 7:117)

"And when the terror fell on them they cried: O Moses! Pray for us unto thy Lord, because He hath a covenant with thee. If thou removest the terror from us we verily will trust thee and will let the Children of Israel go with thee. But when We did remove from them the terror for a term which they must reach, behold! they broke their Covenant" (Quran 7:134-135)

Israel Saved?

Christian Question; All of Israel saved (Romans 11:26) *Vs* Israel not saved (Luke 12:9, John 1:11)

Priest's Excuse; Paul is speaking of the unconditional promise given to Israel;

"I am going to give you and your descendants all the land that you see, and it will be yours forever." (Genesis 13:15)

Muslim Reply: This only expands the contradiction rather than contracts it. If Genesis says Israel will be saved forever, then again this contradicts the Bible which says that Israel will be cursed forever, because once saved (Genesis 13:15), then to reject salvation (Romans 5:9), results in damnation;

"For how can those who abandon their faith be brought back to repent again? They were once in God's light; they tasted heaven's gift and received their share of the Holy Spirit; they knew from experience that God's word is good, and they had felt the powers of the coming age. And then they abandoned their faith! It is impossible to bring them back to repent again, because they are again crucifying the Son of God and exposing him to public shame." (Hebrews 6:4-6)

This is also verified in Bible, which states that Israel can fall out of salvation;

"And Samuel said to him, "The Lord has torn the kingdom of Israel from you this day, and has given it to a neighbor of yours, who is better than you." (1 Samuel 15:28)

In conclusion, the nation of Israel, like everyone else on earth, is judged according to its faith and actions and is blessed or cursed based on the laws and conditions stated by God. Jesus was correct in saying those who reject his prophethood will be rejected in the Afterlife, while Paul was wrong to claim an unconditional salvation towards the nation of Israel, which both Jesus and the Bible rebuff.

Quranic Answer: The Holy Quran explains that each individual is judged for his or her own actions:

"Surely Allah does not do injustice to the weight of an atom, and if it is a good deed He multiplies it and gives from Himself a great reward." (Quran 4:40)

The Holy Quran shows that all nations, either ethnically Jewish or Gentile, will have salvation if they believe in Allah and are righteous:

"Lo! those who believe, and those who are Jews, and Sabaeans, and Christians whosoever believeth in Allah and the Last Day and doeth right there shall no fear come upon them neither shall they grieve." (Quran 5:69)

Hence, people are judged individually, rather than a nation. Furthermore, the Holy Quran confirms that Israel was favored and their prayers were answered as a nation but as in the Bible, fell from its favored status;

"And when there comes to them a Book from Allah, confirming what is with them,- although from of old they had prayed for victory against those without Faith,- when there comes to them that which they (should) have recognized, they refuse to believe in it but the curse of Allah is on those without Faith." (Quran 2:89)

<u>Biblical self hate;</u>

Christian Question; The Bible writers express self disgust at their job in writing the Bible; ". . .ye have perverted the words of the living God. . ." (Jeremiah 23:36)

"How can you say, 'We are wise, and the law of the Lord is with us'? But, behold, the false pen of the scribes has made it into a lie." (Jeremiah 8:8)

" And the Lord said to me: "The prophets are prophesying lies in my name; I did not send them, nor did I command them or speak to them. They are prophesying to you a lying vision, worthless divination, and the deceit of their own minds." (Jeremiah 14:14)

Even Jesus admits the Scribes omitted things from the Bible; "Woe unto you, scribes and Pharisees, hypocrites! for ye pay tithe of mint and anise and cumin, and have omitted the weightier matters of the law, judgment, mercy, and faith: these ought ye to have done, and not to leave the other undone. " (Matthew 23:23)

Priest's Excuse; The scribes were talking about being corrupt on a different religious matter.

Muslim Reply: Interestingly the Christians confess the Bible writers were corrupt, how then can we trust that they were corrupt in some religious matters and not others. Furthermore, the scribes specify that their "pens" turned the words of God into lies.

Quranic Answer: The Quran emits love and self confidence in the writing within:

"We have, without doubt, sent down the Message; and We will assuredly Guard it (from corruption). (Quran: 15:9)

"Say: Were the oceans ink for the Words of my Lord, the ocean would surely fail before the Words of my Lord fail; aye, though We brought as much ink again!" (Quran 18:110)

"No falsehood can approach it from before or behind it: It is sent down by One Full of Wisdom, Worthy of all Praise." (Quran 41:42)

"Nay, this is a Glorious Quran, (inscribed) in a Tablet Preserved! (Quran: 85:21-22)

(E.) WOMEN

Adam or Eve to blame?

Jewish Vs. Christian Question; How does Eve, the mother of all human beings, measure in the Bible compared to the Quran? Assessing the Biblical depiction of Eve reveals the root of negative stereotyping towards women;

"When God asked Adam why he ate from the forbidden tree, he answered, according to the Bible." And the man said, the Woman whom thou gavest to be with me, she gave me of the tree, and I did eat. And the Lord God said unto the woman, what is this that thou hast done? And the woman said, the serpent beguiled me, and I did eat." (Genesis 3:12-13)

"And I will put enmity between thee and the woman, and between thy seed and her seed; it shall bruise the head, and thou shalt bruise his heel. Unto the woman he (God) said, I will greatly multiply thy sorrow and thy conception; in sorrow thou shalt bring forth children; and thy desire shall be to thy husband, and he shall rule over thee." (Genesis 3:15-16)

As we can see in this scenario, Adam played a great part in committing the sin of eating from the forbidden tree, so why was it blamed on Eve?

Priest's Excuse; None available.

Quranic Answer: The Quran gives a non-biased narration, dispelling the gender inequality that the Bible portrays;

"Then did Satan make them slip from the (garden), and get them out of the state (of felicity) in which they had been. We said: "Get ye down, all (ye people), with enmity between yourselves. On earth will be your dwelling-place and your means of livelihood - for a time." (Quran 2:36)

"Then began Satan to whisper suggestions to them, bringing openly before their minds all their shame that was hidden from them (before): he said: "Your Lord only forbade you this tree, lest ye should become angels or such beings as live for ever."

"And he swore to them both, that he was their sincere adviser. So by deceit he brought about their fall: when they tasted of the tree, their shame became manifest to them, and they began to hide (by heaping) on themselves some of the leaves of the Garden."

"And their Lord called them, (saying): Did I not forbid you from that tree and tell you: Lo! Satan is an open enemy to you? They said: "Our Lord! We have wronged our own souls: If thou forgive us not and bestow not upon us Thy Mercy, we shall certainly be lost." (Quran 7:20-23)

In summary, while the Bible solely blames it on Eve, the Quran holds both Adam and Eve responsible and equally forgives both.

Adam and Eve equally punished?

Jewish Vs. Christian Question; A disproportionate amount of Biblical wrath befell Eve in comparison to Adam. Malicious and agonizing punishments were thrust onto Eve, while the Bible maintains Adam's relative innocence.

"And the man said, the woman whom Thou gavest to be with me, she gave me of the tree, and I did eat." (Genesis 3:12) In turn, Eve blames the Serpent for hoaxing her.

Although Adam indirectly guiltily accuses God "Thou gavest to be with me", Eve is unfairly cursed four more times than Adam is. The four additional curses on Eve are delineated in Genesis;

"Unto the woman He said, (1st) I will greatly multiply thy sorrow and (2nd) thy conception; in sorrow thou shalt bring forth children; (3rd) and thy desire shall be to thy husband, and (4th) he shall rule over thee." (Genesis 3:16)

Adam's sin exceeded Eve's in the Biblical enactment because Adam succumbed to temptation quicker and through less influence than Eve endured with the serpent. Adam was reprimanded to a lesser degree, for a larger crime.

"Now the serpent was more subtle than any beast of the field which God had made." (Genesis 3:1)

Adam's scolding was a fraction to Eve's curses. The retributions placed on Adam were in fact additional damnations placed on Eve;

"And unto Adam he said, Because thou hast hearkened unto the voice of thy wife, and hast eaten of the tree, of which I commanded thee, saying, Thou shalt not eat of it: cursed is the ground for thy sake; (1st) in sorrow shalt thou eat of it all the days of thy life"

"Thorns also and thistles shall it bring forth to thee; (2nd)and thou shalt eat the herb of the field; In the sweat of thy face (3rd) shalt thou eat bread, till thou return unto the ground; for out of it wast thou taken: for dust thou art, and unto dust shalt thou return" (Genesis 3:17-19)

We recognize that Adam is given three in contrast to the four curses on Eve. Additional assessment reveals that Adam's dietary curses actually afflict Eve as well. Therefore, Eve suffers four separate curses and jointly shares Adam's three eating maledictions. Paul in the Bible expounds on Eve's curses by saying; "...Adam was not deceived, but the woman was deceived and became a transgressor. Yet woman will be saved through bearing children" (1 Timothy 2:14-15) Paul reiterates the Biblical perspective that Eve was debauched, hence women must suffer for retribution, while Adam, and men owe no supplementary penance.

Priest's Excuse; None available.

Quranic Answer: The Holy Quran counters the fallacious accusations placed on Eve;

"But Satan whispered evil to him: he said, "O Adam! shall I lead thee to the Tree of Eternity and to a kingdom that never decays?" In the result, they both ate of the tree, and so their nakedness appeared to them: both began to cover themselves with leaves of the garden, thus and Adam disobeyed his Lord, so went astray." (Quran 20:120-121)

The Quran expels the chauvinistic accusation that Eve was the lone perpetrator. The Quran also places Adam at the scene of the transgression and acknowledges he also spoke with Satan. Consequently, Adam and Eve were equally punished for their disobedience. In Conclusion, the women in the world are not indebted for any additional deeds towards Salvation, according to the Quran.

<u>Divorce Allowed?</u>

Jewish Vs. Christian Question; Divorce allowed (Deuteronomy 24:1–4) *Vs* Divorce not allowed (Mark 10:1–12) and (1 Corinthians 7:10–16)

Priest's Excuse; That is what it says but that is not what it means. Jesus and Paul were talking about what God wants yet Moses was talking about what actually happens.

Muslim Reply: The problem with this excuse is that Jesus does indeed acknowledge what Moses said and overrides it by saying Moses said this because of a fault within the Jews, but now this fault is punishable by death. The reason Moses allowed divorce is no longer acceptable to anyone; "Whosoever shall put away his wife, and marry another, committeth adultery against her." (Mark 10:11)

"Whosoever", meaning anyone under any condition is not allowed to divorce their wife and visa versa, and if they do divorce their wife, the punishment is death because these perplexing writings claim Jesus equated divorce with adultery and adultery is punishable by stoning to death.

Quranic Answer: In the Holy Quran, God understands that there are many conditions that warrant divorce. Spouses do not have to stay together under a death threat Instead, two married people are allowed to divorce one another after they have attempted to reconcile their differences. God states within the Holy Quran that if a divorce is intended to take place, that each person must wait 4 months before doing as a "waiting" or cooling off" period:

"For those who wish to separate from their wives, then they shall wait four months. If they concede, then God is most forgiving, merciful." (Quran 2:226)

"Once the interim is fulfilled, you may reconcile with them equitably, or go through with the separation equitably. You shall have two equitable witnesses witness the divorce before God. This is to enlighten those who believe in God and the Last Day. Anyone who reverences God, He will create an exit for him." (Quran 65:2)

At any moment during the 4-month interim the divorce may be retracted and the couple may settle their differences.

<u>A Divorcee is an adulteress?</u>

Jewish Vs. Christian Question; A major problem in the Bible is the condemnation of divorcees. Once a woman has been with a man (in a marital relationship) the woman (now divorced) naturally desires to remarry, yet the Bible states that the marriage to a divorcee is punishable by death;

"Whosoever marries a divorced woman commits adultery." (Matthew 5:32)

The Bible contradicts itself in this regard by wording in another section that women are ratified remarriage without repercussion; as Moses says a divorcee "may go and be another man's wife" (Deuteronomy 24:2)

Priest's Excuse; None available.

Quranic Answer: The Holy Quran corrects this degradation and contradiction within the Bible by stating that divorcees are not sinners, instead they are just as honorable as women whom have never been married, for marriage and divorce have no bearing on a woman's character and as such, these divorcees are to be treated in kindness as well as be given permission to remarry:

"A divorce is only permissible twice: after that, the parties should either hold Together on equitable terms, or separate with kindness. It is not lawful for you, (Men), to take back any of your gifts (from your wives), except when both parties fear that they would be unable to keep the limits ordained by Allah. If ye (judges) do indeed fear that they would be unable to keep the limits ordained by Allah, there is no blame on either of them if she give something for her freedom. These are the limits ordained by Allah; so do not transgress them if any do transgress the limits ordained by Allah, such persons wrong (Themselves as well as others)." (Quran 2:229-30)

So if a husband divorces his wife (the third time), He cannot, after that, re-marry her until after she has married another husband and He has divorced her. In that case there is no blame on either of them if they re-unite, provided they feel that they can keep the limits ordained by Allah. Such are the limits ordained by Allah, which He makes plain to those who understand.

Ex-husband's child?

Jewish Vs. Christian Question; In the Bible, Moses is depicted to allow women to immediately remarry after a divorce (Deuteronomy 24:1-2). The error with this broad law is that if a woman immediately remarries, and is unknowingly pregnant, no one will know who the father of the baby is. In contradiction to Moses, Jesus is falsely recorded to have said in the Bible;

"whoever marries a divorced woman commits adultery." (Matthew 5:32)

This was stated seemingly to prevent the spread of fatherless children

Priest's Excuse; None available.

Quranic Answer: The Holy Quran solves the problem of unknown fathers to children of divorcees as created in the Bible, without alienating and punishing the mothers to a life without remarriage as Jesus is claimed to do; "Divorced women shall wait concerning themselves for three monthly periods. Nor is it lawful for them to hide what Allah Hath created in their wombs, if they have faith in Allah and the Last Day. And their husbands have the better right to take them back in that period, if they wish for reconciliation. And women shall have rights similar to the rights against them, according to what is equitable; but men have a degree (of advantage) over them. And Allah is Exalted in Power, Wise." (Quran 2:228)

In order for the identity of the child's father to be known, divorcees must wait 3 months before remarriage, to verify before marrying another whether or not they are pregnant. This method even eliminates today's method of men taking blood tests which leads to the ex-couples fighting and deeming this method to be inaccurate.

Pagan Wives?

Jewish Vs. Christian Question; Divorce pagan wives (Ezra 10:11) *Vs* Do not divorce pagan wives (1 Corinthians 7:12).

Priest's Excuse; 1st) Later Scripture replaces Previous Scripture. 2nd) not all pagans are the same.

Muslim Reply: 1st) If this is true, then over a billion Muslims state that the Quran, which came after the Bible, supersedes past revelations (Torah and Gospel). The fact is, God promised to Abraham that the covenant of Laws is forever and everlasting, as well as Jesus himself declaring he did not come to change the laws; "Do not think that I came to destroy the Law or the Prophets. I did not come to destroy but to fulfill. For verily I say unto you, Till heaven and earth pass, one jot or one title shall in no wise pass from the law, till all be fulfilled. " (Matthew 5:17-18).

Either you do believe in God or you don't, or as the Christians say; you're either saved or not.

Quranic Answer: The Quran clarifies that men are not allowed to marry pagan women:

"Do not marry unbelieving women (idolaters), until they believe: A slave woman who believes is better than an unbelieving woman, even though she allures you. Nor marry (your girls) to unbelievers until they believe: A man slave who believes is better than an unbeliever, even though he allures you. Unbelievers do (but) beckon you to the Fire. But Allah beckons by His Grace to the Garden (of bliss) and forgiveness, and makes His Signs clear to mankind: That they may celebrate His praise." (Quran 2:221)

The Holy Quran settles the difference in the Bible by stating that men are not allowed to marry pagans/atheists but we are allowed to marry people of the Book

"This day are (all) things good and pure made lawful unto you. The food of the People of the Book is lawful unto you and yours is lawful unto them. (Lawful unto you in marriage) are (not only) chaste women who are believers, but chaste women among the People of the Book, revealed before your time, - when ye give them their due dowers, and desire chastity, not lewdness, nor secret intrigues if any one rejects faith, fruitless is his work, and in the Hereafter he will be in the ranks of those who have lost (all spiritual good)." (Quran 5:5)

(F.) JESUS

Mary a Virgin or Young woman?

Jewish Vs. Christian Question; Jews and Christians argue regarding the use of (Isaiah 7:14) as a confirmation to the birth of Jesus;

"Therefore the Lord Himself will give you a sign: Behold, a virgin will be with child and bear a son, and she will call His name Immanuel," (Isaiah 7:14).

Hebrew scholars attest that this passage is speaking of a maiden, not a virgin, thus concluding this is not a prophecy.

The problem is dealing with the Hebrew word for virgin, which is "almah". According to the *Strong's Concordance* it means, "virgin, young woman 1. of marriageable age 2. maid or newly married." Therefore, the word "almah" does not always mean virgin. Additionally, there is a more accurate Hebrew word for virgin: "bethulah".

Priest's Excuse; Both have valid arguments against each other.

Muslim Reply: In the days of Jesus, adultery laws were extremely strict, even deadly. Therefore, unless the maiden was identified as a married woman, then 99% of the time, she was a virgin.

Note; she was not called a harlot or adulterous as unmarried promiscuous women were labeled in the Bible, further proving she is a virgin as the majority of young women were during the days of Jesus.

Quranic Answer: The Quran crystallizes the fact that Mary was a virgin:

"And Mary the daughter of 'Imran, who guarded her chastity; and We breathed into (her body) of Our spirit; and she testified to the truth of the words of her Lord and of His Revelations, and was one of the devout (servants)." (Quran 66:12)

Jesus Demonized?

Jewish Vs. Christian Question; In an apparent oversight within the Bible, Jesus professes that he is Lucifer, a serious flaw absent from the Quran.

Jesus and Satan in the Bible both have the same name; "Morning Star"

"King of Babylon, bright morning star, you have fallen from heaven! In the past you conquered nations, but now you have been thrown to the ground." (Isaiah 14:12)

Even the *KJV OT Hebrew Lexicon* states "morning star" means; Lucifer, light-bearer, king of Babylon and Satan.

Shockingly, The Bible falsifies Jesus as attributing this title to himself;

"I, Jesus, have sent my angel to give witness to you of these things in the churches. I am the root and the offspring of David, the bright and morning star." (Revelation 22:16)

Christians often use this method of self-ascription by Jesus in attempts to prove Jesus' divinity, for example;

"God said to Moses, "I am who I am". This is what you are to say to the Israelites: `I am' has sent me to you.'" (Exodus 3:14)

Christians then link Exodus to try to explain that Jesus is God;

"I tell you the truth," Jesus answered, "Before Abraham was born, I am!" (John 8:58)

By the same Christian logic of transferring descriptive analogies from one character in the Bible to another, Jesus is also personified as Satan.

Priest's Excuse; Mistranslation.

Muslim Reply: Here we see how a mistranslation can transform Jesus from a righteous Prophet into Satan, thus demonstrating the dangers and scope of errors in the Bible.

Quranic Answer: In conclusion, while the Bible mistakenly demonizes Jesus, the Quran calls Jesus: "The statement of the truth" (Quran 19:34), "Servant of God" (Quran 19:31) "The Messiah (Quran 9:31), and "with the spirit from God" (Quran 4:171).

<u>Christ Cursed?</u>

Jewish Vs. Christian Question; Jesus is cursed (Galatians 3:13) *Vs* Jesus is not cursed (Psalms 72:17)

Priest's Excuse; Jesus was both; cursed on earth and blessed in Heaven.

Muslim Reply: The apologists are willing to stoop to new lows to avoid a disparity. It's shocking that they're willing to call their presumed God and savior "Cursed" while the Bible says it's Satan who's the cursed one (Genesis 3:14).

Quranic Answer: The Quran corrects the Biblical insult on Prophet Jesus by saying Jesus was blessed on earth and the Afterlife:

"Behold! the angels said: "O Mary! Allah giveth thee glad tidings of a Word from Him: his name will be Christ Jesus, the son of Mary, held in honor in this world and the Hereafter and of (the company of) those nearest to Allah" (Quran 3:45)

First to be Resurrected?

Jewish Vs. Christian Question; Jesus was the first to be resurrected (1 Corinthians 15:20) *Vs* Others were resurrected before Jesus (1 Kings 17:22; 2 Kings 13:21)

Priest's Excuse; Others were resuscitated while Jesus was resurrected because Jesus was immortal.

Muslim Reply: In an effort to correct a discrepancy, the Biblicists add more contradictions. First, if Jesus were genuinely immortal, then he would not have died in the first place.

Second, the Bible uses the word "resurrected", not "resuscitated" as the apologists would prefer.

Quranic Answer: The Quran corrects the Bible in that it indicates that there have been resurrections before Jesus and never states that Jesus was the only to be resurrected:

"Or (take) the similitude of one who passed by a hamlet, all in ruins to its roofs. He said: "Oh! how shall Allah bring it (ever) to life, after (this) its death?" but Allah caused him to die for a hundred years, then raised him up (again). He said: "How long didst thou tarry (thus)?" He said: (Perhaps) a day or part of a day." He said: "Nay, thou hast tarried thus a hundred years; but look at thy food and thy drink; they show no signs of age; and look at thy donkey: And that We may make of thee a sign unto the people, Look further at the bones, how We bring them together and clothe them with flesh." When this was shown clearly to him, he said: "I know that Allah hath power over all things." (Quran 2:259)

Forgiveness before Jesus?

Jewish Vs. Christian Question; People before Jesus went to Heaven (2 Kings 2:11) *Vs* No one will go to Heaven unless they accept Jesus (John 10:9, 14:6).

Priest's Excuse; The Bible confirms that previous prophets believed in God (James 2:23), which is the same as believing in Jesus.

Muslim Reply: According to Paul, believing in Jesus was not enough; one had to accept the supposed blood sacrifice of Jesus (Romans 5:9) which was impossible for previous people to postulate because Jesus had not yet come to earth.

Quranic Answer: The Holy Quran displays a fair system of salvation, which gives accountability to past and future creations of Allah.

"... No laden soul will bear another's load." (Quran 39:7)

And

"Surely Allah does not do injustice to the weight of an atom, and if it is a good deed He multiplies it and gives from Himself a great reward." (Quran 4:40)

(G.) TRINITY

King of All?

Jewish Vs. Christian Question; There is a multidimensional problem in the Bible with the claim that Jesus is the King of Kings. First, within his lifetime, Jesus never claimed to be the King of Kings, only the King of Jews;

[King of Jews] "Then Pilate asked Him, "Are You the King of the Jews?" He answered and said to him, "It is as you say." (Mark 15:2)

Second, briefly after Jesus claimed to be the King of Jews, he was disproved;

[Invalidated King] "Let the Christ, the King of Israel, descend now from the cross that we may see and believe." Even those who were crucified with Him reviled Him." (Mark 15:32)

Third, after the passing of Jesus, Paul in an attempt to deify him says;

[King of all] "The Lamb will overcome them because he is the Lord of Lords and King of Kings" (Revelation 17:14)

The problem with Paul calling Jesus the King of all is three fold, 1) Jesus never claimed to be the King of all, only of Jews. 2) Jesus supposedly died on the cross, discrediting his Kingship. 3) The title "King of Kings" is already taken by another man;

"Artaxerxes, King of Kings, To Ezra the priest, a scribe of the Law of the God of heaven: Perfect peace, and so forth." (Ezra 7:12)

Therefore, the title "King of Kings" regarding Jesus in the Bible is not only unclaimed and discredited by Jesus, but also conflicts with other "men" who bore that title.

Priest's Excuse; None available.

Quranic Answer: In the Holy Quran, no other living creature as in the Bible [(Ezekiel 26:7), (1 Kings 10:23), (Ezra 7:12) and (Revelation 17:14)], has been called "King of Kings except for God alone:

“High above all is Allah, the King, the Truth! Be not in haste with the Quran before its revelation to thee is completed, but say, “O my Lord! advance me in knowledge.” (Quran 20:114)

And

“All that is in the heavens and all that is in the earth glorifieth Allah, the King, the Holy, the Mighty, the Wise.” (Quran 62:1)

And

“He is Allah, besides Whom there is no god; the King, the Holy, the Giver of peace, the Granter of security, Guardian over all, the Mighty, the Supreme, the Possessor of every greatness Glory be to Allah from what they set up (with Him).” (Quran 59:23)

The Creator?

Jewish Vs. Christian Question; “By him (Jesus) all things were created: things in heaven and on earth, visible and invisible, whether thrones or powers or rulers or authorities.” (Colossians 1:16) *Vs* “(Jesus) who is the image of the invisible God, the firstborn of every creature” (Colossians 1:15) *Vs* “And, behold, thou shalt conceive in thy womb, and bring forth a son, and shalt call his name Jesus.” (Luke 1:31)

There is confusion as to when Jesus was created (either first, as was Adam) or (centuries later through Mary). One thing is clear, that is Jesus was created, and by definition, not the Creator.

Priest’s Excuse; Mistranslation of the Greek word “prototokos” which should read “pre-eminent” instead of “first born”; making Jesus the creator rather than the created.

Muslim Reply: The Bible is riddled with translation errors. The translators can use anyone of the multi-meanings of vague words to insinuate deity to many of the characters in the Bible, including Jesus, the only problem with this insinuation is that it contradicts other parts of the Bible that disprove their divinity.

Quranic Answer: The Holy Quran which is kept authentic in its original language (Arabic) clarifies that Jesus was “created” like Adam:

“The similitude of Jesus before Allah is as that of Adam; He created him from dust, then said to him: "Be". And he was.” (Quran 3:59)

and that only God is the Creator:

"Those who celebrate the praises of Allah, standing, sitting, and reclining, and contemplate the (wonders of) creation in the heavens and the earth, (With the thought): "Our Lord! not for naught Hast Thou created (all) this! Glory to Thee! Give us salvation from the penalty of the Fire." (Quran 3:191)

The Unique?

Jewish Vs. Christian Question; "And the Word was made flesh, and dwelt among us, (and we beheld his glory, the glory as of the only begotten of the Father,) full of grace and truth." (John 1:14) *Vs* David 'also' being a begotten son;

"I will declare the decree: the Lord hath said unto me, Thou art my Son; this day have I begotten thee." (Psalms 2:7)

Priest's Excuse; Biblical commentaries differ among themselves whether David was a manifestation of Jesus or whether David was also a begotten son of God.

Muslim Reply: Every time a character in the Bible has attributes equal to or greater than Jesus (Hebrews 7:3-4), apologists throw away all context for these characters and assert it was another manifestation of Jesus to avoid the fact that Jesus was not unique.

Quranic Answer: God in the Quran unlike the Prophets in the Bible shows there is none like Allah, the Unique Creator:

"And your Allah is One Allah: There is no god but He, Most Gracious, Most Merciful." (Quran 2:163)

The Hidden?

Jewish Vs. Christian Question; "And God said, Thou canst not see my face: for there shall no man see me, and live." (Exodus 33:20) and "No man hath seen God at any time" (John 1:18) *Vs* "Jesus answered him, I spake openly to the world; I ever taught in the synagogue, and in the temple, whither the Jews always resort; and in secret have I said nothing." (John 18:20)

Priest's Excuse; Jesus was not God on earth.

Muslim Reply: Agreed; nor is Jesus (God) in Heaven because God does not lose the "status" of being God wherever God is (Joshua 2:11).

Quranic Answer: The Holy Quran corrects this conflict in the Bible:

"He is the First and the Last and the Ascendant (over all) and the Hidden, and He is Cognizant of all things." (Quran 57:3)

<u>God Afraid of us?</u>

Jewish Vs. Christian Question; "If thou wilt not observe to do all the words of this law that are written in this book, that thou mayest fear this glorious and fearful name, The Lord Thy God; Then the Lord will make thy plagues wonderful, and the plagues of thy seed, even great plagues, and of long continuance, and sore sicknesses, and of long continuance." (Deuteronomy 28:58-59)

And

Jesus speaking about himself according to Trinitarians;

"And fear not them which kill the body, but are not able to kill the soul: but rather fear Him which is able to destroy both soul and body in hell." (Matthew 10:28, Luke 8:50, 12:4)

Vs

"After these things Jesus walked in Galilee: for he would not walk in Jewry, because the Jews sought to kill him." (John 7:1)

"Then they took up stones to cast at him: but Jesus hid himself, and went out of the temple, going through the midst of them, and so passed by." (John 8:59)

And

"While ye have light, believe in the light, that ye may be the children of light. These things spake Jesus, and departed, and did hide himself from them." (John 12:36-37)

From childhood, Jesus hid over 10 years in Egypt to avoid death;

"Now when they were departed, behold, an angel of the Lord appeareth to Joseph in a dream, saying, Arise and take the young child and his mother, and flee into Egypt, and be thou there until I tell thee: for Herod will seek the young child to destroy him." (Matthew 2:13)

Priest's Excuse; 1st) It was not yet his time to die; "My hour has not yet come" (John 2:4; 8:20)

Muslim Reply: We know that Jesus escaped from death during his childhood (Matthew 2:13)

Second, even when it was his so-called time, Jesus, displayed intense fear, crying out twice;

“Jesus again gave a loud cry and breathed his last.” (Matthew 27:50)

In conclusion, whether Jesus was supposed to die as a child or as an adult, every effort was made by him to avoid death.

Quranic Answer: Unlike the Bible, the Quran exhibits a Fearless God;

“O Prophet! Fear Allah, and hearken not to the Unbelievers and the Hypocrites: verily Allah is full of Knowledge and Wisdom.” (Quran 33:1)

“O Ye who believe! Put not yourselves forward before Allah and His Messenger; but fear Allah: for Allah is He Who hears and knows all things.” (Quran 49:1)

Trinitarians Lazy?

Jewish Vs. Christian Question; Trinitarians claim that we no longer have to do the work God commanded us to do. Their reasoning is that (1) we could not do the laws (Romans 3:10) and (2) Jesus was God, and his death on the cross removed past and future sin, so there’s –no longer- any reason to follow the millenniums old, Laws of God;

“For Christ has brought the Law to an end, so that everyone who believes is put right with God.” (Romans 10:4)

“Yet we know that a person is put right with God only through faith in Jesus Christ, never by doing what the Law requires.” (Galatians 2:16)

And

“And so the Law was in charge of us until Christ came, in order that we might then be put right with God through faith.” (Galatians 3:24)

Vs

As we have already shown, and as Trinitarians (contradicting themselves) say, “Jesus was not God on earth”. Besides the divine disqualification for Jesus to replace the laws or remove the sins associated with the laws, there is another obstacle for Trinitarians to claim the laws are "too hard" for us to accomplish;

"you will have to obey him and keep all his laws that are written in this book of his teachings. You will have to turn to him with all your heart. The command that I am giving you today is not too difficult or beyond your reach. It is not up in the sky. You do not have to ask, "Who will go up and bring it down for us, so that we can hear it and obey it?' Nor is it on the other side of the ocean. You do not have to ask, "Who will go across the ocean and bring it to us, so that we may hear it and obey it?' No, it is here with you. You know it and can quote it, so now obey it."

"Today I am giving you a choice between good and evil, between life and death. If you obey the commands of the Lord your God, which I give you today, if you love him, obey him, and keep all his laws, then you will prosper and become a nation of many people. The Lord your God will bless you in the land that you are about to occupy. But if you disobey and refuse to listen, and are led away to worship other gods, you will be destroyed—I warn you here and now. You will not live long in that land across the Jordan that you are about to occupy." (Deuteronomy 30:10-18)

Furthermore, Jesus claimed to have promised many people would be in Heaven before he supposedly ended the Law through his claimed resurrection;

"So then, whoever disobeys even the least important of the commandments and teaches others to do the same, will be least in the Kingdom of heaven. On the other hand, whoever obeys the Law and teaches others to do the same, will be great in the Kingdom of heaven." (Matthew 5:19)

"Happy are those who are persecuted because they do what God requires; the Kingdom of heaven belongs to them!" (Matthew 5:10)

"Happy are those who know they are spiritually poor; the Kingdom of heaven belongs to them!" (Matthew 5:3)

"but Jesus said, "Let the children come to me, and do not hinder them; for to such belongs the kingdom of heaven." (Matthew 19:14)

Last, Jesus himself taught that following the commandments and the laws is the way to salvation;

"Not every one that saith unto me, Lord, Lord, shall enter into the kingdom of heaven; but he that doeth the will of my Father which is in heaven." (Matthew 7:21)

Priest's Excuse; The laws were supposed to be followed until the resurrection, but after the resurrection, the laws were done away with;

"Purge out therefore the old leaven, that ye may be a new lump, as ye are unleavened. For even Christ our Passover is sacrificed for us" (1 Corinthians 5:7)

Muslim Reply: It is a faulty notion to claim the laws, which were followed for millenniums, were only made to be temporary. Both the God of Abraham and Jesus state the laws are forever;

"Everlasting" ,"For All Generations", "a Perpetual Ordinance " (Exodus 27:21; 28:43; 29:28; 30:21; 31:17; Leviticus 6:18, 22; 7:34, 36; 10:9, 15; 17:7; 23:14, 21, 41; 24:3; Numbers 10:8; 15:15; 18:8, 11, 19, 23; 19:10; Deuteronomy 5:29; Psalms 119:160) and is Not to be changed or taken away from (Deuteronomy 4:2; 12:32).

Jesus confirms the Laws are for all generations and everlasting by following the laws (Matthew 8:4, 26:19, John 7:10).

Actions speak louder than words and besides the actions of Jesus keeping the Everlasting Laws, Jesus also states;

"Think not that I am come to destroy the law, or the prophets: I am not come to destroy, but to fulfill. For verily I say unto you, Till heaven and earth pass, one jot or one title shall in no wise pass from the law, till all be fulfilled." (Matthew 5:17-18)

In conclusion, God, the Prophets, and the Messiah all say the Laws are unending. The Righteous have one enemy, he who leads people astray through lethargy.

Quranic Answer: God through the Holy Quran explains that it is a combination of Faith and Works that gives us Salvation:

"For Him (alone) is prayer in Truth: any others that they call upon besides Him hear them no more than if they were to stretch forth their hands for water to reach their mouths but it reaches them not: for the prayer of those without Faith is nothing but (futile) wandering (in the mind)." (Quran 13:14)

The Holy Quran explains that works are to our benefit:

"O you whose hearts have been touched with the divine hand: When you intend to stand before God for performing your act of worship, then ablution becomes a duty. Wash your faces, your hands and the forearms up to the elbows, and with your wet hands wipe your heads, then wash your feet to the ankles...God does not intend to put you in difficulty but only to make you sound headed men of proper discipline and excellent mind, and to set you upon a course of purity of thought and action, for the actions of men are best interpreters of their thoughts, and He means to make all grace abound in you that you may hopefully actuate yourselves with the feeling of gratitude and gratefulness and lift Him your inward sight." (Quran 5:6)

Worshipping a man?

Jewish Vs. Christian Question; The majority of Christians believe that Jesus is God in flesh form, hence these Christians worship Jesus. These Christians validate worshipping Jesus, through the following verses;

"And when they were come into the house, they saw the young child with Mary his mother, and fell down, and worshipped him: and when they had opened their treasures, they presented unto him gifts; gold, and frankincense, and myrrh." (Matthew 2:11)

"And as they went to tell his disciples, behold, Jesus met them, saying, All hail. And they came and held him by the feet, and worshipped him." (Matthew 28:9)

"And changed the glory of the incorruptible God into an image made like to corruptible man" (Romans 1:23)

Yet the Bible also says;

"I am the Lord, that is my name; my glory I give to no other, nor my praise to graven images." (Isaiah 42:8)

And

"For I am the Lord; I change not." (Malachi 3:6)

And

"God is not a man, that he should lie; neither the son of man, that he should repent." (Numbers 23:19)

Priest's Excuse; None available.

Quranic Answer: The confusion of whether to worship or not to worship a man is resolved through the Quran:

"And behold! Allah will say "O Jesus the son of Mary! didst thou say unto men `worship me and my mother as gods in derogation of Allah?" He will say: "Glory to Thee! never could I say what I had no right (to say). Had I said such a thing Thou wouldst indeed have known it. Thou knowest what is in my heart though I know not what is in Thine. For Thou knowest in full all that is hidden."

Clearly, we should only worship God and God alone.

"Never said I to them aught except what Thou didst command me to say to wit `Worship Allah my Lord and your Lord'; and I was a witness over them whilst I dwelt amongst them; when Thou didst take me up thou wast the Watcher over them and Thou art a Witness to all things." (Quran 5:116-117)

In conclusion, the Trinitarians propagate that Jesus, the Holy Spirit, and God are all 100% equal, and are all a part of the triune God. These Christians try to justify this notion with the mathematical equation (1 X 1 X 1=1) yet according to the excuses of the Bible scholars; the value of Jesus is not completely equal to God.

By their own admission, Jesus on earth was (<) less than God in heaven.

Therefore, the actual equation is (.5 X .5 X 1=.25) Symbolically, by claiming Jesus is a part of a trinity, the triune god becomes a fraction.

(H.) AFTERLIFE

How to remove Sin?

Jewish Vs. Christian Question; Christians ask if the only way to salvation is through blood; " For the life of the flesh is in the blood: and I have given it to you upon the altar to make an atonement for your souls: for it is the blood that maketh an atonement for the soul." (Leviticus 17:11)

Vs

Multiple methods of removing sin; giving charity (Exodus 30:15-16) and (Numbers 31:50), incense (Numbers 16:46-47)

Priest's Excuse; None available.

Quranic Answer: Islam teaches that there is no one single way to salvation for salvation comes from both works and faith:

"For Him (alone) is prayer in Truth: any others that they call upon besides Him hear them no more than if they were to stretch forth their hands for water to reach their mouths but it reaches them not: for the prayer of those without Faith is nothing but (futile) wandering (in the mind)." (Quran 13:14)

"They will say: "Did there not come to you your messengers with Clear Signs?" They will say, "Yes". They will reply, "Then pray (as ye like)! But the prayer of those without Faith is nothing but (futile wandering) in (mazes of) error!" (Quran 40:50)

"Those who believe, and do deeds of righteousness, and establish regular prayers and regular charity, will have their reward with their Lord: on them shall be no fear, nor shall they grieve." (Quran 2:277)

Born sinners?

Jewish Vs. Christian Question; Children are born pure, without sin (Leviticus 11:44, 19:2, 20:7) *Vs* Children are born wicked sinners (Psalms 58:3)

Priest's Excuse; That is what it says but that is not what it means. (Psalms 58:3) is speaking about the potential to commit sin, not being an actual sinner.

Muslim Reply: The language and context used is that of one who is a sinner, not of one who will be a sinner.

"The wicked are estranged from the womb" -not- "will be" (future tense), instead "are" (present tense)

"they go astray as soon as they be born, speaking lies."

This is not stating that they will go astray as adults but as soon as they are born. Furthermore, Paul also adopts the absurdity that children are sinners by claiming;

"Wherefore, as by one man sin entered into the world, and death by sin; and so death passed upon all men, for that all have sinned" (Romans 5:12)

Quranic Answer: The Quran corrects the fallacy that children are inherently evil or have contracted sin of previous generations;

"We have indeed created man in the best of moulds." (Quran 95:4)

"Every soul draws the wages of its acts on none But itself: no bearer of burdens can bear The burden of another." (Quran 6:164)

"...No laden soul will bear another's load. Then unto your Lord is your return; and He will tell you what ye used to do. Lo! He knoweth what is in the breasts (of men)." (Quran 39:7)

Who is Satan?

Jewish Vs. Christian Question; There is confusion in the Bible as to whether Satan is a fallen angel or not; Satan is free to act as he pleases (Job 1:6-7, 2:1-2, Matt 4:1, 1 Pet 5:8) *Vs* The angels who rebelled against God are chained up (Jude 6)

Priest's Excuse; 1st) That is what it says but that is not what it means. The angels will be ultimately bound in the future, but are not yet actually bound;

"And, behold, they cried out, saying, What have we to do with thee, Jesus, thou Son of God? art thou come hither to torment us before the time?" (Matthew 8:29)

2nd) There are two different types of fallen angels, those in chains and those not.

Muslim Reply: 1st) Here the Bible scholars attempt another word play by confusing the past, current and future tense of the passages;

"For if God spared not the angels that sinned, but cast them down to hell, and delivered them into chains of darkness, to be reserved unto judgment" (2 Peter 2:4)

We see the past tense verbs are "spared not, sinned, cast them down, delivered, and reserved" It is obvious to any reader that the fallen angels were thrown out past tense, are chained up current tense, and will be judged future tense.

2nd) "...spared not the angels that sinned..." (2 Peter 2:4) proves that none of the angels who sinned were spared, instead of some of the angels as the apologists suggest. Nothing suggests that there are two different types of fallen angels except for the contradiction that evil angels are free to roam and yet at the same time are chained up.

Quranic Answer: The Noble Quran specifies that Satan was a Jinn (a separate breed of creatures made from fire (15:27), not an Angel:

"Behold! We said to the angels, "Bow down to Adam": They bowed down except Iblis. He was one of the Jinns, and he broke the Command of his Lord. Will ye then take him and his progeny as protectors rather than Me? And they are enemies to you! Evil would be the exchange for the wrong-doers!" (Quran 18:50)

Reap what you sow?

Jewish Vs. Christian Question; Do we reap what we sow? Some sow wheat but reap thorns. (Jeremiah 12:13) *Vs* Some sow but will not reap anything. (Micah 6:15) *Vs* Some reap without sowing. (Matthew 25:26, Luke 19:22) *Vs* A man reaps what he sows. (2 Corinthians 9:6, Galatians 6:7)

Priest's Excuse; The first are materialistic sowing, thus uneven, the last is afterlife spiritual sowing, thus even.

Muslim Reply: This would be acceptable albeit for the passage stating that the righteous reap what they sow in this life, hence materialistic terms;

"Behold, the righteous shall be recompensed in the earth: much more the wicked and the sinner." (Proverbs 11:31) because (Matthew 25:26, Luke 19:22) speaks of the wicked materialistically getting more than the righteous.
Therefore, even if it is in materialistic terms, it is in contradiction to (Proverbs 11:31)

Quranic Answer: The Quran is very clear that humans get what they deserve. In an accountable fashion, God is Fair and Bountiful. People are punished for the bad deeds they commit or mercy from our Lord is upon them and either way, they are greatly rewarded for the good:

"Surely Allah does not do injustice to the weight of an atom, and if it is a good deed He multiplies it and gives from Himself a great reward." (Quran 4:40)

Righteous Immortal?

Jewish Vs. Christian Question; The righteous in the Bible are immortal; "No grave trouble will overtake the righteous" (Proverbs 12:21) *Vs* the righteous in the Bible are mortal;

"…How can ye escape the damnation of Hell? Wherefore, behold, I send unto you prophets, and wise men, and scribes: and some of them ye shall kill and crucify; and some of them shall ye scourge in your synagogues, and persecute them from city to city: That upon you may come all the righteous blood shed upon the earth, from the blood of Innocent Abel unto the blood of Zacharias son of Barachias, whom ye slew between the temple and the altar. Verily I say unto you, All these things shall come upon this generation." (Matthew 23:33-36)

Priest's Excuse; (Proverbs 12:21) is speaking about only a few righteous people, not all righteous people.

Muslim Reply: We know that the Bible has universally taught the false concept that the righteous are immortal. This is based from other passages stating such;

"They shall take up serpents; and if they drink any deadly thing, it shall not hurt them; they shall lay hands on the sick, and they shall recover." (Mark 16:17 – 18)

In an affront to Bible defenders, Mark teaches that all the righteous can drink snake venom and survive, avoiding death. This is a direct contradiction with all the righteous recorded in the Bible who have died.

Quranic Answer: The Quran clarifies that all humans, good or bad, are not immortal:

"Say: "Running away will not profit you if ye are running away from death or slaughter..." (Quran 33:16)

"We have ordained death among you and We are not to be outrun" (Quran 56:60)

Medicine and machines may have the ability to slow the process of death, by the Will of God, but eventually as described in the Quran, we will all die, and the angel of death will come to all of us and we will not be able to prevent the angel from taking us away from this earth.

Earth Forever?

Jewish Vs. Christian Question; "A generation goes, and a generation comes, but the earth remains forever." (Ecclesiastes 1:4, Psalms 78:69, 104:5) *Vs* "Heaven and earth will pass away, but my words will not pass away." (Luke 21:33, 2 Peter 3:10).

Priest's Excuse; Mistranslation. The word "forever" should actually be "long time".

Muslim Reply: We know the word should be something else because it is a mistake the way it is, but to pick and choose what it should be is just as bad. This is an example of how the errors in the Bible range from finite to infinity.

Quranic Answer: The Holy Quran confirms that the earth will not last forever; instead, there will be a day when the earth is destroyed:

"And when the earth is spread out And hath cast out all that was in her, and is empty" (Quran 84:3-4)

Unconditional Love?

Jewish Vs. Christian Question; The Bible teaches that God will love the sinners (Matthew 5:43-45, Romans 5:6 – 10, 8:38–39) *Vs.* God will not love the sinners (Hosea 9:15);

"I hated them: for the wickedness of their doings I will drive them out of mine house, I will love them no more: all their princes are revolters."

Priest's Excuse; None available.

Quranic Answer: It would be a punishment on the Righteous if God loved the sinners, because then the Judgment of God would have no equitable value, and Heaven would be intertwined evil murderers along with their victims, making the potential of more violence and revenge in the Afterlife. Instead, God in the Quran is a fair Judge and gives love to those who do not reject the love of God:

"That He may reward those who believe and work righteous deeds, out of his Bounty. For He loves not those who reject Faith." (Quran 30:45)

(2.) Questions on the New Testament

(A.) Prophets

Prophet or Spirit?

Christian Question; There is confusion in the Bible regarding Jesus' criterion;

"I have yet many things to say unto you, but ye cannot bear them now. Howbeit when he, the Spirit of truth, is come, he will guide you into all truth: for he shall not speak of himself; but whatsoever he shall hear, that shall he speak: and he will show you things to come." (John 16:12-13)

While Jesus is clearly speaking of a person, Christians claim Jesus is foretelling the Holy Spirit.

Many see (John 16:12-13) as one of the many predictions of Prophet Muhammad (pbuh) and the -prediction- of the Holy Quran as this book further makes evident.

Priest Answer: That is what it says but that is not what it means. John 16:12-13 is a prediction about the Holy Spirit, not Muhammad pbuh).

Muslim Reply: First, Trinitarians claim that the Holy Spirit, God, and Jesus are all one entity while Jesus was obviously speaking of someone other than himself in (John 16:12-13). Jesus spoke about himself in (v12) "I have" then switches from personal pronouns "I" to "he", rather then maintaining a constant personal pronoun of "I". Jesus does not say; "I will come later to finish speaking".

Secondly, we know that the Holy Spirit and Jesus are not one in the same because of (Matthew 12:31);

"Wherefore I say unto you, all manner of sin and blasphemy shall be forgiven unto men: but the blasphemy against the Holy Ghost shall not be forgiven unto men."

Yet after the thief next to Jesus on the cross –mocked and reviled- Jesus (Mark 15:32), Jesus forgave one and said you will go to Heaven (Luke 23:43).

Third, Jesus admits that he has nothing else to say; Jesus states that everything his Creator wanted him to say was already said;

"for all things that I have heard of my Father I have made known unto you." (John 15:15)

Which confirms an individual other than Jesus will say more. For example; it would be a symptom of schizophrenia for someone to say; "I said everything I was told, and I will come to say more from me and I will glorify myself and I will say nothing of my own will other than what I was told by myself".

One has a free choice of following the Trinitarians' perplexity or believing that (John 16:12-13) was the logical prediction of Prophet Muhammad (pbuh) because our loving God would not leave us for over 2,000 years with no other guidance.

Quranic Answer: (John 16:12-13) was indeed predicting Muhammad (pbuh) for Allah states it within the final revelation, the Holy Quran.

"...whom they will find described in the Torah and the Gospel (which are) with them. He will enjoin on them that which is right and forbid them that which is wrong. He will make lawful for them all good things and prohibit for them only the foul..." (Quran 7:157)

Indeed, we find this is the exact description of Prophet Muhammad (pbuh), foretold in the Bible, who came as a mercy to the worlds to send the final revelation.

(B.) Science

Why Do We Die?

Christian Question; In the Bible, Paul claims we die because of sin. Paul asserts that the first human sinned, therefore lost immortality, and subsequently caused all humans to be seemingly 'cursed' with death.

Paul blames Adam by saying ; "Wherefore, as by one man sin entered into the world, and death by sin; and so death passed upon all men, for that all have sinned" (Romans 5:12)

"For since by man came death, by man came also the resurrection of the dead. For as in Adam all die..." (1 Corinthians 15:21-22)

"Nevertheless death reigned from Adam to Moses, even over them that had not sinned..." (Romans 5:14)

"For the wages of sin is death....." (Romans 6:23)

"It is appointed for men to die once" (Hebrews 9:27)

Priest Answer: Jesus abolished death, but has not gotten the chance to actually do so yet.

Muslim Reply: Either the claimed crucifixion had a great significance or not, either it removed death or not; which by the fact that we still must die, then the answer is that the supposed crucifixion had no significance.

Paul did not truly know if Jesus removed death or not because Jesus had not died yet and it would be the Day of Judgment the day Jesus would come back, which would be too late for any of us to know.

Apparently Paul gained false confidence in defeating death by boldly preaching contradictory Gospels to both Jewish and Gentilian camps while briefly evading assassination, hence his false inspiration to make unfounded remarks regarding death.

Quranic Answer: The Holy Quran shows us that death is a natural process and does not give us episodes of the 'original sin'. The Holy Quran gives us facts from our Creator that we shall only live for a certain period and then return to Allah:

"And among His Signs in this: thou seest the earth barren and desolate; but when We send down rain to it, it is stirred to life and yields increase. Truly, He Who gives life to the (dead) earth can surely give life to (men) who are dead. For He has power over all things." (Quran 41:39)

"Lo! Allah (it is) Who splitteth the grain of corn and the date-stone (for sprouting); He brings forth the living from the dead and He is the bringer forth of the dead from the living; that is Allah! How are you then turned away." (Quran 6:95)

Oxygen, the common cause of death is a natural element, which also helps in the corrosion of automobiles and flowers. The same reaction this element has towards metals and wild life, it too has towards our bodies, slowly aging us until death. This gas is a slow poison that affects each one differently as it also deteriorates metals and plants at various speeds.

As recommended by Doctors in the field of health and medicine, anti-Oxidants are shown to slow the aging process. Nonetheless, the anti-Oxidants do not stop our expiration date, and eventually, at a set time, we all die.

Nearly 1,400 years ago, prior to scientists confirming that the origin of death is the prolonged exposure to the elements on earth, the Holy Quran in these verses compares us to other living organisms. Summarizing that it is a common cycle for the earth to be barren, then brought back to life by Allah.

Therefore, the reason for death is not because of a sin or a curse, yet it is because of the environmental conditions of earth as stated in the Holy Quran. Roses are at one point in full bloom, and as the wilting process takes affect, the rose plant deteriorates and is eventually lifeless, the rose was not born a sinner as we are not born sinners.

This concrete evidence again shows that natural death is not a transmitted curse; instead, death is a natural geological process.

"Every soul shall have a taste of death: and We test you by evil and by good by way of trial. To Us must ye return." (Quran 21:35)

Signifying that death is universal, and no soul is exempt, the word "taste" here supports the fact that common death is due to our life term of inhaling oxygen-based gases.

"Yet have they taken, besides Him, gods that can create nothing but are themselves created; that have no control of hurt or good to themselves; nor can they control death nor life nor resurrection." (Quran 25:3)

It is precisely stated in this verse that neither humans nor created idols that are perceived as gods, can have any control over death, dying is an unavoidable necrosis and those who assumed human or petrified gods could make a human body immortal, were dead wrong.

The Quran debunks all fallacies of these ancient flesh god parables who give us immortality through sacrifices or ritual drinks, for dying is as an unavoidable occurrence as the sun setting is:

"And He it is Who gives life and causes death, and (in) His (control) is the alternation of the night and the day; do you not then understand?" (Quran 23:80)

The Divinity of this cycle is clear. If the sun did not set, and the night did not cover the land, then all of the earth would become barren, and with a constant sun 24 hours a day, the earth would wither away.

Similarly, if humans did not die, the resources on this earth would have been depleted. Humans give birth, which maintains our existence, so factually, both death and birth, maintains our presence here on earth.

Many cycles are referenced to within the Holy Quran which generates and preserves life on our planet, if any of the numerous sequences, including death, were removed from the repeated phenomenon's, the human race would fade away within a century.

If we observe our surroundings realistically, we need death and cannot exist without it. Life and death are as perfect a pair as day and night:

"And all things We have created by pairs, that haply ye may reflect." (Quran 51:49)

(C.) LAWS

Talking to Others?

Christian Question; Do not say anything to a non-believer (2 John 1:10 – 11) *Vs* Always answer a non-believer (1 Peter 3:15)

Priest Answer: These two passages are speaking of two different groups of people.

Muslim Reply: The only difference is in the authors of the passages who both clearly express everyone and do not limit the speaking laws to an elite group.

Quranic Answer: In the matter of theological discussions, we are not asked to ostracize ourselves as in the Bible. Instead, it is just the opposite, we are told to communicate with non-believers:

"Invite (all) to the Way of thy Lord with wisdom and beautiful preaching; and argue with them in ways that are best and most gracious: for thy Lord knoweth best, who have strayed from His Path, and who receive guidance." (Quran 16:125)

Divorced man's rights?

Christian Question; One of the problems in the Bible is the condemnation of divorced men. Once a man has been with a woman (in a marital relationship) the man (now divorced) naturally desires to remarry, yet the Bible states that the marriage to a divorced man is punishable by death;

"He said to them, "A man who divorces his wife and marries another woman commits adultery against his wife." (Mark 10:11)

Divorce here is being acquainted with adultery and adultery is punishable by stoning to death.

Priest's Excuse; None available.

Quranic Answer: The Holy Quran corrects this confinement in the Bible by stating that it is permissible for divorced men to remarry:

"A divorce is only permissible twice: after that, the parties should either hold Together on equitable terms, or separate with kindness. It is not lawful for you, (Men), to take back any of your gifts (from your wives), except when both parties fear that they would be unable to keep the limits ordained by Allah. If ye (judges) do indeed fear that they would be unable to keep the limits ordained by Allah, there is no blame on either of them if she gives something for her freedom. These are the limits ordained by Allah; so do not transgress them if any do transgress the limits ordained by Allah, such persons wrong themselves as well as others." (Quran 2:229-30)

So if a husband divorces his wife (the third time), He cannot, after that, re-marry her until after she has married another husband and He has divorced her. In that case, there is no blame on either of them if they re-unite, provided they feel that they can keep the limits ordained by Allah. Such are the limits ordained by Allah, which He makes plain to those who understand.

Thus, it is not sinful for a man or woman to be divorced and remarry.

Self Amputation?

Christian Question; The Bible allows and even promotes self amputation;

"For there are some eunuchs, which were so born from their mother's womb: and there are some eunuchs, which were made eunuchs of men: and there be eunuchs, which have made themselves eunuchs for the kingdom of heaven's sake. He that is able to receive it, let him receive it. (Matthew 19:12)

"Wherefore if thy hand or thy foot offend thee: cut them off, and cast them from thee." Matthew 18:8

Priest's Excuse; The Bible was speaking figuratively

Muslim Reply: Thousands throughout Christian history have become eunuch monks based on the motivation from the Bible. Earlier Christians believed those passages to be speaking literally, thus followed the literal advice. Furthermore, (Matthew 19:12) emphasizes the meaning is literal because it gives the example of those who are born eunuchs and then states those that become like them will have paradise. Although modern Christians may have secularized out of this early Christian norm, self amputation is still a well documented Christian phenomenon.

Quranic Answer: The Holy Quran teaches us to preserve and love ourselves:

"And spend of your substance in the cause of Allah, and make not your own hands contribute to (your) destruction; but do good; for Allah loveth those who do good." (Quran 2:195)

“O ye who believe! Eat not up your property among yourselves in vanities: But let there be amongst you Traffic and trade by mutual good-will: Nor kill (or destroy) yourselves: for verily Allah hath been to you Most Merciful! (Quran 4:29)

Islam teaches to pray and perform fasting to avoid temptations, rather than the horrid self amputation taught in the Bible.

"And seek assistance through patience and prayer, and most surely it is a hard thing except for the humble ones" (Quran 2:45)

Biblical Suicide?

Christian Question; The Bible does not contain any laws against suicide, and instead has an abundant amount of characters (Mostly Prophets), wishing for and committing suicide without any rebuke or punishment for their suicidal tendencies;

Moses was in despair because of the complaints of the Israelites whom he was leading. The burden of leadership was too heavy for him to bear. He asked God "If You treat me like this, please kill me here and now..." (Numbers 11:12-15)

Samson had been chained to the two middle pillars of a temple. He pushed them apart. thereby knowingly causing the collapse of the building, and his own suicide. (Judges 16:29-30)

In a war against the Philistines, Saul's sons Johnathan, Abinadab and Malchishua were killed, and Saul himself was seriously wounded. He asked his armor bearer to kill him, but his assistant refused. So he took a sword and fell on it. The armor bearer then also fell on his sword. Both committed suicide. (1 Samuel 31:4-6)

In an act of vicious religious intolerance, Elijah ordered 400 priests of Baal executed. Ahab went to Jezebel, telling her that Elijah had "executed all the prophets with the sword." She swore to kill Elijah within the next 24 hours. Elijah fled for this life to Beersheba, went into the wilderness, and "prayed that he might die." He said, "It is enough! Now, LORD, take my life, for I am no better than my fathers!" (1 Kings 18:40 and 19:4)

God had threatened the destruction of the Nineveh, a city of 120,000 people. But the king and people of the city listened to Jonah, repented of their sins, and fasted. God changed his mind and did not destroy the city. Jonah was so angry at God's display of mercy that he asked God to kill him, "for it is better for me to die than to live!" He repeated the same request to God on the next day. (Jonah 4:1-11)

Even in the Gospel; Paul is contemplating whether it is better to live or die. He is hard pressed to decide between the two, "having a desire to depart and be with Christ, which is far better. Nevertheless to remain in the flesh is more needful for you...yet what I shall choose I cannot tell." (Philippians 1:20-26)

More Biblical suicides; (1 Kings 16:18), (2 Samuel 17:1-29), (Judges 9:52-54), (Matthew 27:5), (Revelation 9:1-10).

Priest's Excuse; 1st) the Bible says "Thou shalt not kill." 2nd) the Bible says "Do not be a fool--why die before your time?" (Ecclesiastes 7:17b)

Muslim Reply: 1st) The vague commandment "Thou shalt not kill" obviously cannot be interpreted literally, because people continually kill plants and animals for food. The context is interpreted as meaning that one should not murder another human being.

2nd) According to the "*Jamieson, Fausset, Brown Bible Commentary*", (Ecclesiastes 7:17b) is warning God will be provoked to cut off prematurely thy day of grace (Romans 2:5), thus not a warning against suicide, furthermore, the context states in passage (7:15) that a wicked man can have a prolonged life, thus (7:17) is simply saying that the wicked should not feel safe as also explained in the *"Matthew Henry Complete Commentary on the Whole Bible"*.

Quranic Answer: The Holy Quran does directly and specifically tell us to love ourselves by not killing ourselves;

"And spend of your substance in the cause of Allah, and make not your own hands contribute to (your) destruction; but do good; for Allah loveth those who do good." (Quran 2:195)

"O ye who believe! Eat not up your property among yourselves in vanities: But let there be amongst you Traffic and trade by mutual good-will: Nor kill (or destroy) yourselves: for verily Allah hath been to you Most Merciful! (Quran 4:29)

(D.) WOMEN

Women Allowed to Speak?

Christian Question; The Bible states: "The women should be silent in the churches, for they are not permitted to speak. Rather, let them be in submission, as in fact the law says. If they want to find out about something, they should ask their husbands at home." (1 Corinthians 14:34-35).

"Let the woman learn in silence with all subjection. But I suffer not a woman to teach, nor to usurp authority over the man, but to be in silence." (1 Timothy 2:11-15)

The Bible also forbids women from speaking in a church (1 Corinthians 14:34-35).

Priest's Excuse; That is what it says but that is not what it means. Apologists assert that remaining silent in those verses actually meant being submissive. Otherwise, men and women are equally redeemed;

"there is neither male nor female; for you are all one in Christ Jesus" (Galatians 3:28)

Muslim Reply: Paul obviously did not mean submissiveness when he said for women to be silent because in (I Timothy 2:8) Paul says for women to be both submissive and silent, hence debunking the notion that Paul only meant submissive when he also stated for women to 'be silent'. Again, the apologists try to twist the meanings of words by ignoring the context of the words used;

"But I suffer not a woman to teach" and "nor to usurp authority over the man." (1 Timothy 2:12)

The excuse actually shows how Paul contradicts himself within the Gospel even further, whereas in one instance the Bible tells women to keep silent and in another instance, the Bible foretells women prophesizing (Acts 2:17).

The apologists err even further when they try to dig up passages where Paul likens men to women, in one passage Paul says women and men are saved equally (Galatians 3:28), while in another passage, Paul claims that have to stomach a different redemption;

"And Adam was not the one who was deceived; it was the woman who was deceived and became a sinner. But women will be saved through childbearing." (1 Timothy 2:14-15)

Quranic Answer: Within the Quran, you will not find a single verse that states a woman cannot speak during any particular time, let alone not at all! In fact, the Quran states the following:

"Indeed Allah has heard the statement of her that disputes with you (O Muhammad) concerning her husband and complains to Allah. And Allah hears the argument between you both. Verily Allah is All-Hearer, All Seer." (Quran 58:1)

Not only does this woman, Khaulah bint Tha'labah, speak with the Prophet (pbuh) but she is even arguing with him, and The Most Merciful, Allah, is listening to them both! The woman is not being condemned for speaking her mind and heart to the Prophet (pbuh) and disputing with him over a matter, yet instead, Allah is reassuring that He hears this woman's complaints and that He is the All-Hearer of all people, men, and women.

<u>Who are Eve's parent?</u>

Christian Question; According to the Christian's logic regarding the relationship of Jesus to God, children who are born with only one parent must have God as the other parent. This argument would be logical except for the fact that Eve, who only had one parent, is not considered the daughter of God as Jesus is considered the son of God.

The similarities between Jesus and Eve are almost identical;

Mary's womb was barren and childless similar to Adam's rib, childless and barren. Also, Adam's rib made Eve and Mary's womb made Jesus.

Priest's Excuse; None available.

Quranic Answer: The womb and the rib were used as a tool by Allah to Create.

Eve was born from another human as Jesus was born from another human; Jesus was born with the help of Allah as Eve was born with the help of Allah. Allah creates, and does not beget.

"There is no god but He: It is He Who gives life and gives death, - The Lord and Cherisher to you and your earliest ancestors." (Quran 44:8)

"He begetteth not nor was begotten." (Quran 112:3)

"The similitude of Jesus before Allah is as that of Adam; He created him from dust, then said to him: "Be". And he was." (Quran 3:59)

(E.) JESUS

Two Blind Men?

Christian Question; Jesus heals two blind men on the way to Jericho. (Matthew 20:29-34) *Vs* He heals one blind man. (Mark 10:46-52)

Priest's Excuse; Although Mark says one, he could have meant two.

Muslim Reply: Curing one blind person may have been coincidental, but curing two blind men is an absolute miracle, and for Mark to ignore the second time a man was supposedly cured or just focus on one and ignore the other is the similitude of a person ignoring the sun being eclipsed.

Furthermore, in other situations where there were two individuals, Mark mentions "both";

"And with him they crucify two thieves; the one on his right hand, and the other on his left." (Mark 15:27) & (Mark 15:32)

Quranic Answer: The Quran clarifies that Jesus was given the power by God to heal blind people, and hence, Jesus could have healed more than one or two people, for he had that power God bestowed upon him to heal people (plural).

"and thou (Jesus) healest those born blind, and the lepers, by My leave." (Quran 5:110)

Beyond a Reasonable Doubt?

Christian Question; The Quran answers questions in regards to the claimed crucifixion of Jesus and here we will witness one of the phenomenal expansive statements that covers and resolves an entire episode.

The Quran demystifies the disorder in the Bible surrounding the crucifixion of Jesus. For over 2,000 years, the Bible editors have been stressed to harmonize the following eighteen tensions that the Quran relieves with one single verse.

Allah, the Reckoner through the Quran, debunks the presumptive evidence in the Bible by showing that there is a reasonable doubt.

Jesus answers no charges at his hearing before Pilate. (Matthew 27:11-14) *Vs* Jesus answers all charges at his hearing before Pilate. (John 18:33-37)

Were the allegations answered?

Priest's Excuse; None available.

Quranic Answer: In the next fifteen questions, the answer is miraculously summarized by one verse from the Holy Quran before humans even knew that the questions were present.

Allah, being the Ultimate Authority, has issued a verdict settling the crucifixion incident;

"That they said (in boast), "We killed Christ Jesus the son of Mary, the Messenger of Allah"; - but they killed him not, nor crucified him, but so it was made to appear to them, and those who differ therein are full of doubts, with no (certain) knowledge, but only conjecture to follow, for of a surety they killed him not" (Quran 4:157)

Therefore, the Quran proves what Bible editors have been trying to hide, based on the differing testimonies from Mark, Matthew, Luke, and John.

If the Christians love Jesus as much as they claim, the Christians would not insist Jesus was killed with all the conflicting evidence surrounding the murder, especially since he was found alive a few days later.

<u>Too Heavy?</u>

Christian Question; Who bore the cross? They compelled Simon to bear the cross of Jesus. (Matthew 27:32), (Luke 23:26) & (Mark 15:21) *Vs* Jesus was bearing the cross himself. (John 19:17)

Priest's Excuse; Bible proponents pursue to rationalize this disparity by proposing Jesus collapsed after the flogging and interrogation, at which point Simon persisted to carry the cross. The problem with this assumed scenario is more questions now arise with not enough answers.

Muslim Reply: First, if Jesus did indeed fall, and did not carry the cross, why didn't any of the disciples document the "fall of Jesus"? Second, if John did indeed delete the detail of Jesus being too decrepit, in order to demonstrate divinity; doubt develops regarding what other erasures have taken place discrediting the deity of Jesus? While on the other hand, it is only in the testimony of John do we find derogatory statements suggesting Jesus is divine. Third, less minor details are mentioned in the Gospel of John, i.e. (the exact hour Jesus was placed on the cross John 19:14), etc... How then could the occurrence of a fellow disciple (Simon), participating in the crucifixion of Jesus be disregarded?

We realize the suggestion that the disciple John "left out" this occurrence is unacceptable, casting an even larger shadow of distrust on John's Biblical narration.

Quranic Answer: (Quran 4:157)

<u>What did they put Jesus on?</u>

Christian Question; In (Mark 15: 32) we are told that Jesus was put on a "cross" to be crucified:

"Let Christ the King of Israel descend now from the cross, that we may see and believe. And they that were crucified with him reviled him."

The word used here for "cross" in the Greek edition is "stauros", yet in (1 Peter 2:24) we are told that Jesus was crucified on the "tree":

"Who his own self bare our sins in his own body on the tree, that we, being dead to sins, should live unto righteousness: by whose stripes ye were healed."

The word in this verse for "tree" in the Greek edition is "xulon"

Priest's Excuse; Bible proponents pursue to rationalize this disparity by proposing a mistranslation from the Greek text, but as we witnessed, even the verses in Greek use differing words to describe the wooden object allegedly used to defeat Jesus. Yes, both a tree and a cross can be equally used as a stake, stick, staff, for all words are related in the lexicon meaning of the two, yet this relationship does not excuse the fact that two different words were used. A tree and a cross can also have completely opposite dictionary meanings. Hence, showing an equal degree of difference in the meanings.

Muslim Reply: First, suggesting a mistranslation of the Bible from Greek is unacceptable because Christians claim the Bible is divine and that the Bible is the exact word of God in every language. Second, both the words used in Greek are themselves divergent and their meanings are not identical. Third, such an explanation tries to bridge elements from their primal to their completed state, which is a long process absent between the passages. For example "he was killed with a rock" or "he was killed with a sculpture", two contradictory weapons, depicting unreliable witnesses.

Quranic Answer: (Quran 4:157)

My Father or Abba?

Christian Question; What did Jesus call God while allegedly on the cross? "My Father" (Matthew 26:39) *Vs* "Abba" (Mark 14:36)

Priest's Excuse; Mistranslation.

Muslim Reply: Again, Bible apologists want us to believe the Bible is 100% inerrant when they themselves admit that the transmitters also made copying errors. This is another unacceptable excuse because it is admitting the Bible we have today has human errors, hence not a divine book.

Quranic Answer: (Quran 4:157)

Final Prayer?

Christian Question; There is a riddle regarding the last words before the reputed crucifixion. Did Jesus indeed pray to God to prevent the excruciation?

"And going a little farther he fell on his face and prayed, "My Father, if it be possible, let this cup pass from me; nevertheless, not as I will, but as thou wilt." (Matthew 26:39)

Here we see Jesus was praying to be saved;

"And he said, "Abba, Father, all things are possible to thee; remove this cup from me; yet not what I will, but what thou wilt." (Mark 14:36)

"Father, if thou art willing, remove this cup from me; nevertheless not my will, but thine, be done." (Luke 22:42)

The major problem lies in John's testimony;

"Now is my soul troubled. And what shall I say? 'Father, save me from this hour'? No, for this purpose I have come to this hour." (John 12:27)

Jesus denies he will pray to be saved

Note; the quote in the narration of John is during the Passover Festival at the Temple in Jerusalem, before the trial by Pharisees.

The key problem here is that John portrays Jesus both denying he will pray and then actually omitting the prayer of Jesus during the crucifixion. In (John 19:16-30), there is no prayer as the other three disciples documented. Instead, a strong and silent Jesus is illustrated.

We conclude that based on the four stories; there is a web of lies. If we start from the first three pupils and compare them with Jesus in the gospel of John denying he will pray for salvation, then all three made a false testimony. Yet if all three actually did see Jesus ask for deliverance, then John was the false witness because he claimed Jesus would not make the plea and disregarded the wish when it was made. This is an ongoing bolstering attempt by John, characterizing a Jesus that can lift the cross by himself without the help of Simon and does not need God's help either while on the cross.

Priest's Excuse; Apologists say that Jesus nobly yet unenthusiastically faced death.

Muslim Reply: The problem with this excuse is that John claims Jesus did eagerly face death because that was his whole purpose for being; Jesus was waiting his whole life for that moment and was not about to spoil it by asking to be saved;

"Now is my soul troubled. And what shall I say? 'Father, save me from this hour'? No, for this purpose I have come to this hour." (John 12:27)

So, do we have a brave Jesus in the Gospel of John ready to face being oppressed and killed or do we have a Jesus who was not only unenthusiastic to face what the oppressors wanted to do to him but also was praying for God's help in the other three Gospels.

Quranic Answer: (Quran 4:157)

<u>The last word?</u>

Christian Question; Another alteration is the alleged last words of Jesus before he died;

"Father, into thy hands I commit my spirit!" (Luke 23:46) *Vs* "It is finished" (John 19:30).

Priest's Excuse; 1st) Bible proponents pursue to rationalize this disparity by proposing the proximity of the two disciples distorted their descriptions. 2nd) Another attempted explanation is that Luke used the last words that he felt were necessary for his Gospel ount, which concentrated on the humanity of Jesus. While John, under duress, twisted the words of Jesus for the fulfillment of the salvific message.

Muslim Reply: 1st) This is excusable for two witnesses of a traffic accident giving opposing accounts due to where they observed the event from. Yet it is unacceptable to excuse differing accounts between Bible authors asserting they are documenting the words of God. 2nd) This claim possesses more questions than answers, similar to John deleting who carried the cross.

The intentional adding, deleting, or altering of the words or actions of Jesus to appease one's own personal interpretation of the character of Jesus is blasphemy and should therefore be named "Luke's or John's opinion of the Bible", rather than "the Bible". For instead of having an actual recording, we are left with conjectures, hypotheses, and as the Bible defenders admit, self-satisfying alterations. In conclusion, the distinction shows a lack of respect on both authors, trading the precise presumed last dying words of Jesus in exchange for their own gluttony.

Quranic Answer: (Quran 4:157)

<u>See You in Heaven?</u>

Christian Question; A premature promise to paradise [Friday] was the day pledged to the partnering prisoner (Luke 23:43), yet on [Sunday] Jesus states he has not yet gone to Heaven (John 20:17).

Priest's Excuse; 1st) The time period peculiarity between Friday and Sunday is often blamed on punctuation between Greek and English, further insulting our Creator by pretending God took part in improper pronunciations. 2nd) That is what it says but that is not what it means. The Spirit of Jesus went immediately to Heaven but his body did not.

Muslim Reply: 1st) The excuse of a mistranslation or mis-punctuation is unacceptable in the light of the final revelation, the Holy Quran.

Apologists admit that some of the errors in the Bible are attributed to translation errors from Hebrew to Greek to German to English. Of course, any linguist would also admit that no word could be perfectly translated from one language to another, especially from one language funneled down through four languages.

This may be acceptable in earthly texts, but this excuse is unacceptable in Divine Scripture, especially in the light of the Quran. This excuse is corrected by the Quran because the Quran is only accepted as authentic in its original language (Arabic). Yet, Bible apologists want us to still believe that the Bible is Divine and inerrant in every language of the world, and at the same time confess that there are translation errors in the Bible, when that is linguistically impossible.

2nd) If Jesus meant his body had not gone up yet, then he would have specified his body instead of stating "I" (as a whole) has not gone to the Father yet. The Gospel speaks of the body over 120 times;

"thy whole body should be cast into hell." (Matthew 5:29)

Jesus differentiates between himself and his body often;

"This is my body which is given for you" (Luke 22:19)

So it is inexcusable that he does not mention or does not specify that only his body did not see God yet as the Bible defenders assert.

Another reason why the (spirit only) excuse is faulty is that according to Christians, Jesus was God, so their spirit was already together, therefore there was no reason for the spirit only to ascend, and their supposed full reunion to be on Sunday as Jesus is claimed to have said.

The third reason this excuse is invalid is that it would be accusing Jesus of being a liar! If his inner self (soul/spirit) already ascended to God and came back, then Jesus would be a liar to say, "I have not yet ascended to My Father".

Quranic Answer: (Quran 4:157)

<u>When did the curtain fall?</u>

Christian Question; Did Jesus die before the curtain of the temple was torn?

Yes (Matthew 27:50-51; Mark 15:37-38) *Vs* No (Luke 23:45-46).

Priest's Excuse; Luke wrote the events in reverse order.

Muslim Reply: This is a selective rational, while disregarding that the rest of Luke's Gospel is not written in reverse order. Therefore, we cannot accept that just this part is in reverse to pardon the contradiction and ignore the rest of Luke's chronological order.

Quranic Answer: (Quran 4:157)

The hours?

Christian Question; Was Jesus on the cross at the sixth hour (Mark 15:33) *Vs* (John 19:14) In Pilate's court at the sixth hour.

Also

"It was the third hour, and they crucified him." (Mark 15:25) *Vs* "It was the sixth hour, and he was not yet crucified" (John 19:14)

Priest's Excuse; Matthew, Mark, and Luke used a different system of numbering the hours of day (Hebrew) opposed to John (Roman).

Muslim Reply: First, John was just as Jewish as the other three Gospels. Naturally, they would all use the same time format. For example, Americans all use "miles" to measure distance, and would not use "kilometers".

Second, it appears that John was not using a different time format, instead a different (time zone). While it was still daytime in the other Gospels (Mark 14:12-17), it was night time for John;

"He then having received the sop went immediately out: and it was night." (John 13:30)

Third, to appease apologists, we will assume for a moment that John did use the Roman time format. What the Christians ignore is that the Romans divided the night into four 3-hour watches, whereas the Jewish format divided the night into three 4-hour watches.

(Matthew 14:25) "And in the fourth watch of the night, he [Jesus] came to them, walking upon the sea."

(Mark 6:48) also says, "fourth watch", both indications that Matthew and Mark used the Roman format too. Therefore, if John used the Roman format, so did Matthew and Mark, which proves the discrepancy exists.

Fourth, Christian scholars disagree that the error comes from a difference between the Roman and Jewish time format;

According to the *Adam Clarke Commentary* (Mark 15:25), the passage (John 19:14) should read "the third hour" and that a manuscript error is involved.

Quranic Answer: (Quran 4:157)

Eulogy?

Christian Question; "And when the centurion, who stood facing him, saw that he thus breathed his last, he said, "Truly this man was the Son of God!" (Mark 15:39) and (Matthew 27:54) *Vs* "Now when the centurion saw what had taken place, he praised God, and said; "Certainly this man was innocent!" (Luke 23:47)

Priest's Excuse; "This is a mistranslation in the Bible.

Muslim Reply: A translation error is the same as saying it's a misquotation error, meaning one of the writers misheard what was being said, which is also as bad as saying the writer miswrote what was being written, regardless of the filter being used to record the information, one of those filters did not function properly, causing the process to fail.

Quranic Answer: (Quran 4:157)

Confirmation of Death?

Christian Question; Joseph of Arimathea asks Pilate for Jesus' body, and Pilate is unaware of whether he is dead; only after sending a centurion and receiving this confirmation does he allow Joseph to take the body. (Mark 15:43-45) *Vs* Pilate actually authorizes the leg breaking to ensure they have all died and then authorizes Joseph to remove the body. (John 19:31-33, 38)

Priest's Excuse; None available.

Quranic Answer: (Quran 4:157)

Nights of Burial?

Christian Question; Jesus to be buried for three days and nights (Matthew 12:40) *Vs* Jesus buried for one day and two nights (Mark 15:42, 43, John 20:1)

Priest's Excuse; That is what it says but that is not what it means. Bible scholars stretch far to try to rectify this problem. These Bible scholars go as far as saying that a day in this particular verse does not mean a full 24 hour day.

Muslim Reply: What the apologists are not grasping is that whether a day is shortened or extended by a day, one of the two conflicting verses will still be inconsistent with the other;

If one day equals to 12 hours instead of 24, then there is still a conflict with (Matthew 12:40) who says 3 days while (John 20:1) says 1. And if we were to extend the days, the same conflict would remain. If we are expected to believe a day is shorter in one verse, then consequently we have to shorten the days in the entire Bible; which would cause the 1 *Vs* 3 days problem to still be there.

The confusion may stem from the disciples not truly knowing if Jesus was really buried at all?

Quranic Answer: (Quran 4:157)

Who told?

Christian Question; A young man in a white robe told the women where Jesus was (Mark 16:5) *Vs* "Two men . . . in dazzling apparel" later described as angels (Luke 24:4 and 24:23). *Vs* Mary met no one and returned saying, "They have taken the Lord out of the tomb, and we do not know where they have laid him" (John 20:2).

Priest's Excuse; Mary Magdalene having seen the tomb opened (John 20:1); she returned to tell the disciples, while the other two women at the tomb went in and saw the angels.

Muslim Reply: Actually, the apologists are ignoring the fact that the women saw the angel roll away the rock (Matthew 28:2-5) so if Mary Magdalene saw the tomb open, she inescapably saw the angel open the tomb as the other two saw this, for how can someone miss seeing an angel moving a boulder, unless the accounts are inaccurate.

Quranic Answer: (Quran 4:157)

Touched?

Christian Question; Mary and the other women met Jesus on their way back from their first and only visit to the tomb. They took hold of his feet and worshipped him (Matthew 28:9) *Vs* Mary met Jesus on her second visit to the tomb. When she saw Jesus, she did not recognize him. She mistook him for the gardener. She still thinks that Jesus' body is laid to rest somewhere and she demands to know where. However, when Jesus said her name she at once recognized him and called him "Teacher". Jesus said to her, "Do not hold me . . ." (John 20:11 to 17).

Priest's Excuse; Only men's testimonies were legal in the first century, thus, we have incomplete accounts, not all of the women's testimonies were recorded because they were not legally legitimate in those days.

Muslim Reply: Then why record it at all in the Bible and causing discrepancies? The accounts are not only incomplete, they are inaccurate. One account tells of Jesus being touched, held, and worshiped and the other tells of Jesus not even being recognized and instructing not to be touched.

Quranic Answer: (Quran 4:157)

Different Bodies?

Christian Question; Jesus appeared in a different body after the resurrection (Mark 16:12) *Vs* Jesus did not appear in a different body after the resurrection (Luke 24:34)

Priest's Excuse; This is a copyist error within the Bible. (Mark 16:9-20) is not found in many ancient manuscripts.

Muslim Reply: Similar to the translation errors or any other errors, a copyist error equally distorts the meaning beyond recognition or comprehension or validity.

Quranic Answer: Bible scholars confirm that their eyes were made to see a different person rather than Jesus (Luke 24:16). This adds to the perplexity in the Bible because if Jesus looked like someone else, then inevitably the person on the cross was someone made to appear to be Jesus, since Jesus was made to appear as someone else. This makes perfect sense in the Quran; otherwise, there would be no logical explanation for Jesus to be formed like someone else in the cave. (Quran 4:157)

Jesus Heard?

Christian Question; Are prayers answered according to the Bible, namely with one of the most righteous Prophets; Jesus?

The humble will be answered;

"If My people who are called by My name will humble themselves, and pray and seek My face, and turn from their wicked ways, then I will hear from heaven, and will forgive their sin and heal their land." (2 Chronicles 7:14)

The earnest and pure will be answered;

"If you would earnestly seek God and make your supplication to the Almighty, if you were pure and upright, surely now He would awake for you, and prosper your rightful habitation." (Job 8:5-6)

The fearful will be answered;

"He will fulfill the desire of them that fear him: he also will hear their cry, and will save them." (Psalms 145:19)

The righteous will be answered;

"The Lord is far from the wicked: but he hears the prayer of the righteous." (Proverbs 15:29)

Even Jesus himself teaches prayers will be answered;

"But you, when you pray, go into your room, and when you have shut your door, pray to your Father who is in the secret place; and your Father who sees in secret will reward you openly." (Matthew 6:6)

Everyone's prayers will be answered;

"Ask and it will be given to you; seek and you will find; knock and the door will be opened to you. For everyone who asks receives; he who seeks finds; and to him who knocks, the door will be opened." (Matthew 7:7-8)

If two pray together their prayers will be answered;

"if two of you on earth agree to ask anything at all, it will be granted to you by my Father in heaven." (Matthew 18:19)

The believers will be answered;

"If you believe, you will receive whatever you ask for in prayer." (Matthew 21:22)

Worshippers will be answered;

"The Lord said, "Now we know that God does not hear sinners; but if anyone is a worshiper of God and does His will, He hears him." (John 9:31)

We see that in general the righteous will be granted redemption upon supplication.

We then see Jesus praying for God to extricate him;

"And going a little farther he fell on his face and prayed, "My Father, if it be possible, let this cup pass from me; nevertheless, not as I will, but as thou wilt." (Matthew 26:39), (Mark 14:36), and (Luke 22:42)

Here, Jesus facing execution prays to God for freedom, yet contrary to all the promises that the righteous will be saved; Jesus' desperate prayer is shown to be forsaken within the Bible;

"With a loud cry Jesus died." (Mark 15:37) and (Matthew 27:50)

Here Jesus cries a second time, with no words recorded, and dies, while in Luke and John, contrary words were reported, yet the outcome was the same, death.

"Jesus cried out in a loud voice, "Father! In your hands I place my spirit!" He said this and died." (Luke 23:46) Or "Jesus drank the wine and said, "It is finished!" Then he bowed his head and gave up his spirit." (John 19:30)

In three of the four Gospels, Jesus cried at least once and prayed to be saved. In two of the four Gospels, Jesus cried a second time. In all four Gospels, Jesus appeared to have died, displaying neglect on the part of God in regards to the prayers of Jesus.

Adding insult to injury, because of this apparent unanswered prayer in the Bible, Jesus is portrayed as a disbelieving and doubtful man, wishing to be rescued, then lashing out when rejected;

"And about the ninth hour Jesus cried with a loud voice, "Eli, Eli, la'ma sabach-tha'ni?" that is, "My God, my God, why hast thou forsaken me?"" (Matthew 27:46)

Non-Christian religions see this unanswered prayer as a disqualification of Jesus, meaning, he did not fit the criteria to be saved, while the Quran teaches the supplication of Jesus was answered.

Priest's Excuse; God wanted Jesus to die, which is why the prayers of Jesus to be saved were not answered.

Muslim Reply: What? Here is where Christian apologists confuse the Bible even more. On the one hand Christians claim Jesus is God, and as we have read, Jesus obviously wanted to be saved. However, in order to explain the contradiction, the Christians try to have it both ways by saying at that moment, Jesus was not God, and the Real God did not want Jesus saved. They try to have their cake (sacrifice) and eat it too (salvation). Christians claim that their trinity is One God, if so, how could their 'One God' want two different things at that same moment? Here we uncover their fallacy because you cannot have One God fighting Himself to live.

Quranic Answer: Allah, being the Ultimate Authority, has issued a verdict settling the crucifixion incident;

"That they said (in boast), "We killed Christ Jesus the son of Mary, the Messenger of Allah"; - but they killed him not, nor crucified him, but so it was made to appear to them, and those who differ therein are full of doubts, with no (certain) knowledge, but only conjecture to follow, for of a surety they killed him not" (Quran 4:157)

Therefore, the Quran proves what Bible editors have been trying to hide, based on the differing testimonies from Mark, Matthew, Luke, and John.

If the Christians love Jesus as much as they claim, the Christians would not insist Jesus was killed with all the conflicting evidence surrounding the murder, especially since he was found alive a few days later.

Turn cheek?

Christian Question; Jesus said, "do not defend yourselves" (Matthew 5:39, Matthew 26:52) *Vs* Jesus said, "defend yourselves" (Luke 22:36)

Priest's Excuse; Some Biblical words are being taken literally instead of symbolically or metaphorically. "turn the other cheek." Figuratively meant, "be moral".

Muslim Reply: Actually, turn the other cheek was a literal commandment because Jesus himself demonstrated this law;

"When he had said this, one of the officers standing by struck Jesus with his hand, saying, "Is that how you answer the high priest?" Jesus answered him, "If I have spoken wrongly, bear witness to the wrong; but if I have spoken rightly, why do you strike me?" (John 18:22-23)

Rather than attacking the officer Jesus reasons with the guard.

This means that if your enemy strikes or attacks you, you are to allow him or her to attack you without striking back. You are to take the punishment without reacting. If the Christians in history allowed themselves to be attacked without retaliating as Jesus claimed to have ordered, than there would not be any Christians left today.

Quranic Answer: The Quran saves the Bible regarding this supposed rule given by Jesus, by clarifying that when you are being attacked, it is best to have patience and forgiveness against the attack, but if the attacks continue, then we are given the permission to retaliate only with the equal amount of force that was used against us:

"And if you take your turn, then retaliate with the like of that with which you were afflicted; But if ye endure patiently, verily it is better for the patient." (Quran 16:126)

Therefore, we are given the permission to repel attacks and to protect ourselves, although Allah prefers forgiveness.

<u>Filled with the Spirit?</u>

Christian Question; Jesus was filled with the Holy Spirit after death (John 7:39) *Vs* Jesus was filled with the Holy Spirit before birth (Luke 1:41, 67)

Priest's Excuse; None available.

Quranic Answer: The Holy Quran teaches all of us that Jesus was a messenger and his mission was to teach and spread the message of Allah. His mission was not to be killed and become a Holy Spirit.

"O People of the Book! Commit no excesses in your religion: Nor say of Allah aught but the truth. Christ Jesus the son of Mary was (no more than) a messenger of Allah, and His Word, which He bestowed on Mary, and a spirit proceeding from Him…" (Quran 4:171)

<u>Jesus Judges?</u>

Christian Question; Jesus judges (John 5:22, 27, 9:39) *Vs* Jesus does not judge (John 3:17, 8:15, 12:47)

Priest's Excuse; Jesus the man does not Judge, but Jesus who will return in his second coming will judge.

Muslim Reply: When the Bible claimed Jesus judges, it does not specify "during the second coming", thus, the contradiction remains.

Quranic Answer: The Quran teaches that Ultimate Judgment belongs to Allah alone, not Jesus:

"And if there is a party of you which believeth in that wherewith I have been sent, and there is a party which believeth not, then have patience until Allah judge between us. He is the Best of all who deal in judgment." (Quran 7:87)

"And (O Muhammad) follow that which is inspired in thee, and forbear until Allah give judgment. And He is the Best of Judges." (Quran 10:109)

Did Jesus lie?

Christian Question; According to the Bible, Jesus is recorded as committing a lie;

"(Jesus said) "Go to the festival yourselves. I am not going to this festival, for my time has not yet fully come." After saying this, he remained in Galilee; but after his brothers had gone to the festival, he went also, not openly, but in secret." (John 7:8-10)

Priest's Excuse; Jesus did not go in the fashion the brothers wanted him to, they wanted Jesus to go openly and Jesus went privately.

Muslim Reply: The issue is not the walking technique of Jesus, the subject is that Jesus stated, "I'm not going", and as soon as the brothers left, Jesus broke his word and went.

Quranic Answer: The Quran holds Jesus in high honor:

"Behold! the angels said: "O Mary! Allah giveth thee glad tidings of a Word from Him: his name will be Christ Jesus, the son of Mary, held in honor in this world and the Hereafter and of (the company of) those nearest to Allah" (Quran 3:45)

"Such (was) Jesus the son of Mary: (it is) a statement of truth, about which they (vainly) dispute." (Quran 19:34)

Witness True?

Christian Question; The testimony of Jesus was true (John 8:14) *Vs* The testimony of Jesus was false (John 5:31)

Priest's Excuse; All men are liars, thus Jesus the man was a false witness before the Jews, but Jesus the God was a true witness.

Muslim Reply: Here the apologists give us more confusion. A liar cannot be an honest man. And an honest man is not a liar. Yes, an honest man can lie but it would be degrading to call God a liar or –false witness-.

Quranic Answer: The Holy Quran explains that Jesus was not God but that his witness is true. Jesus is assigned by Allah in the Quran to be a witness and never states that Christ's witness is false:

"And there is none of the People of the Book but must believe in him before his death; and on the Day of Judgment he will be a witness against them;" (Quran 4:159)

Sent to World?

Christian Question; Do not preach to the Samaritans (Matthew 10:5-6) *Vs* Preach to the Samaritans (John 4:4-41, Acts 8:5, 14, 15, 25)

Priest's Excuse; Both verses are correct; at first Jesus came for Jews only, after the Jews rejected Jesus and the assumed resurrection, they were to preach to the Gentiles as Paul explains;

"to the Jew first, and also to the Greek" (Romans 1:16)

Muslim Reply: There are multiple problems with this excuse

First, why not go to the gentiles from the start, especially when Jesus spent 10 years in Egypt (Matthew 2:13-23).

Second, Christians claim Jesus is God, and the Bible says that God does not change His mind (1 Samuel 15:29); Therefore Jesus cannot go from cursing gentiles to saving them.

Third, When Jesus was presumably resurrected, he could have traveled around the world preaching, yet instead he juststayed in Israel

Fourth, after the resurrection and even after Jesus left the earth, the disciples were still instructed not to preach to gentiles (Acts 11:2-3)

Quranic Answer: The Quran clarifies that Jesus was only sent to the children of Israel:

"And remember, Jesus, the son of Mary, said: "O Children of Israel! I am the messenger of Allah (sent) to you, confirming the Law (which came) before me, and giving Glad Tidings of a Messenger to come after me, whose name shall be Ahmad." But when he came to them with Clear Signs, they said, "this is evident sorcery!" (Quran 61:6)

"And behold! I did restrain the Children of Israel from (violence to) thee when thou didst show them the clear Signs, and the unbelievers among them said: 'This is nothing but evident magic.'" (Quran 5:110)

Shepherd or Sheep?

Christian Question; Jesus is a Shepherd (John 10:11) *Vs* Jesus is a sheep (John 1:29)

Priest's Excuse; Jesus was both and he guided people to accept his sacrifice.

Muslim Reply: If Jesus came to be a Shepherd, he would have taught for the rest of his natural life, and if he came to be a sacrifice (sheep), he would have allowed himself to be caught and killed when he was being chased at childhood (Matthew 2:14) because a sacrificial lamb is only valid as a child;

"You may choose either a sheep or a goat, but it must be a one-year-old male" (Exodus 12:5)

Quranic Answer: The Quran tells us that Jesus came as a Shepherd (teacher and Prophet) with the intentions of giving wisdom, not shedding blood:

"When Jesus came with clear proofs (of Allah's Sovereignty), he said: I have come unto you with wisdom, and to make plain some of that concerning which ye differ. So keep your duty to Allah, and obey me." (Quran 43:63)

Descended to Hell?

Christian Question; Did Jesus descend to Hell;

"For Christ also hath once suffered for sins, the just for the unjust, that he might bring us to God, being put to death in the flesh, but quickened by the Spirit: By which also he went and preached unto the spirits in prison; Which sometime were disobedient, when once the longsuffering of God waited in the days of Noah, while the ark was a preparing, wherein few, that is, eight souls were saved by water." (1 Peter 3:18–20)

Note; (1 Peter 3:18–20) is reiterated in the (Apostles' Creed) as "[Jesus] who was conceived of the Holy Spirit, born of the Virgin Mary, suffered under Pontius Pilate, was crucified, died, buried and descended into hell."

Vs

Jesus ascended to Heaven (Luke 23:43)

Priest's Excuse; The doomed in (1 Peter 3:18 – 20) were angels in Heaven that Jesus tried to save; therefore Jesus went to Heaven, not Hell.

Muslim Reply: To claim Jesus was trying to save angels to avoid the embarrassing Biblical claim that Jesus descended to Hell rather than Heaven, is an affront to the obvious Bible passages and creed that say otherwise. Selective reading will not grant escape from Jesus descending to Hell in the Bible.

First, the reason why the unsaved souls in (1 Peter 3:18–20) were not angels is because they were from "days of Noah, while the ark was being prepared". We know that angels were created before men (Job 38:4-7).

Second, we know that Jesus was not rescuing unsaved angels in Heaven because according to the Bible; Heaven is a place for the righteous while the abode for unsaved angels is "Hell" (Matthew 25:41).

In (2 Peter 2:4), the imprisoned angels are in "Tartarus", a Greek word used to describe a place 'Lower than Hell'. Therefore, in an effort to defend Jesus from being in Hell, they have exposed Jesus to be in "Tartarus", a place lower than Hell.

Note; Some Christians try to insinuate that the Holy Quran suggests that Jesus will go to Hell because those who worship idols and their idols will go to Hell (Quran 21:98) yet Jesus never worshipped Idols nor ever asked to be worshipped. The Jesus in the Gospel is different from the Jesus in the Quran for within the final revelation there is no ambiguity concerning the entity of Jesus. Jesus will not go to Hell, because Muslims do not worship the Jesus.

Quranic Answer: The Quran corrects the Biblical insult on Prophet Jesus by saying Jesus went to Heaven, not Hell:

"Nay, Allah raised him up unto Himself; and Allah is Exalted in Power, Wise" (Quran 4:158)

First Born?

Christian Question; "(Jesus) who is the image of the invisible God, the firstborn of every creature" (Colossians 1:15) *Vs* "By him (Jesus) all things were created: things in heaven and on earth, visible and invisible, whether thrones or powers or rulers or authorities." (Colossians 1:16)

There is confusion as to when Jesus was created (either first, as was Adam) or (centuries later through Mary). One thing is clear and that is Jesus was created, and by definition, not the Creator.

Priest's Excuse; Mistranslation of the Greek word "prototokos" which should read "pre-eminent" instead of "first born"; making Jesus the creator rather than the created.

Muslim Reply: If there is one mistranslation on the status of Jesus, how do we know that there aren't other mistranslations regarding his so-called divinity. If the context shows Jesus being a man who never said "I am God", then we must conclude that any passages that suggest Jesus is God are the real mistranslations.

Quranic Answer: The Quran teaches that Adam was the first-born and that Jesus was made in a similar fashion to Adam's creation:

"It is He Who has created you from a single person (Adam), and (then) He has created from him his wife (Eve), in order that he might enjoy the pleasure of living with her. ..." (Quran 7:189)

"The similitude of Jesus before Allah is as that of Adam; He created him from dust, then said to him: "Be". And he was." (Quran 3:59)

Mary a Sinner?

Christian Question; Protestants argue against Catholics regarding the status of Mary, Because Mary prayed for a Savior, Protestants argue she was a sinner (Luke 1:46) *Vs* Catholics argue Mary was sinless (Luke 1:28)

Priest's Excuse; Both have valid arguments against each other.

Quranic Answer: The Holy Quran corrects multiple misconceptions concerning the mother of the Messiah. The Quran confirms that Mary was made pure.

"Behold! the angels said: "O Mary! Allah hath chosen thee and purified thee- chosen thee above the women of all nations." (Quran 3:42)

Hypocrite?

Christian Question; The Bible insults Jesus by portraying him as a hypocrite. Jesus in the Bible says; 'Anyone who calls another a fool is liable to Hell'. (Matthew 5:22) while shortly afterwards, Jesus says that anyone who hears his words and does not do them is a fool. (Matthew 7:26)

Moving forward, (Matthew 23:17-19) Jesus twice calls the Pharisees blind fools. (Matthew 25:2-3, 8) Jesus compares the maidens who took no oil to fools. Thus, Jesus hypocritically commits the same sin he preached against in the Bible.

Priest's Excuse; That is what it says but that is not what it means

Muslim Reply: The word "fool" has no dual meaning. Whether the phrase is said angrily or softly, (which Jesus was claimed to have said in both tones), the word still has the same meaning.

Quranic Answer: God clears Jesus of hypocrisy in the Holy Quran. The Quran clarifies that Jesus was upright, honorable, and spoke the Good News from Allah, not profanity:

"I have come unto you with wisdom, and to make plain some of that concerning which ye differ. So keep your duty to Allah, and obey me." (Quran 43:63)

"Then We caused Our messengers to follow in their footsteps; and We caused Jesus, son of Mary, to follow, and gave him the Gospel, and placed compassion and mercy in the hearts of those who followed him. But monasticism they invented. We ordained it not for them. Only seeking Allah's pleasure, and they observed it not with right observance. So We give those of them who believe their reward, but many of them are evil livers." (Quran 57:27)

"O ye who believe! Be Allah's helpers, even as Jesus son of Mary said unto the disciples: Who are my helpers for Allah? They said: We are Allah's helpers. And a party of the Children of Israel believed, while a party disbelieved. Then We strengthened those who believed against their foe, and they became the uppermost." (Quran 61:14)

Abolished the Laws?

Christian Question; Jesus did not come to abolish the law. (Matthew 5:17-19, Luke 16:17) *Vs* Jesus did abolish the law. (Ephesians 2:13-15, Hebrews 7:18-19)

Priest's Excuse; The laws were supposed to be followed until the resurrection, after the resurrection, the laws were done away with;

"Purge out therefore the old leaven, that ye may be a new lump, as ye are unleavened. For even Christ our Passover is sacrificed for us" (1 Corinthians 5:7)

Muslim Reply: It is a faulty notion to claim the laws, which were followed for millenniums, were only made to be temporary. Both the Lord of Abraham and Jesus state the laws are forever;

"Everlasting" ,"For All Generations", "a Perpetual Ordinance " (Exodus 27:21; 28:43; 29:28; 30:21; 31:17; Leviticus 6:18, 22; 7:34, 36; 10:9, 15; 17:7; 23:14, 21, 41; 24:3; Numbers 10:8; 15:15; 18:8, 11, 19, 23; 19:10; Deuteronomy 5:29; Psalms 119:160) and is not to be changed or taken away from (Deuteronomy 4:2; 12:32).

Jesus confirms the Laws are for all generations and everlasting by following the laws (Matthew 8:4, 26:19, John 7:10).

Actions speak louder than words and besides the actions of Jesus keeping the Everlasting Laws, Jesus also states;

"Think not that I am come to destroy the law, or the prophets: I have not come to destroy, but to fulfill. For verily I say unto you, Till heaven and earth pass, one jot or one title shall in no wise pass from the law, till all be fulfilled." (Matthew 5:17-18)

In conclusion, the Lord of Abraham in the Bible, the Prophets, and the Messiah all say the Laws are unending. The Righteous have one Enemy, he who leads people astray through lethargy.

Quranic Answer: Allah through the Holy Quran explains that it is a combination of Faith and Works and the Mercy from our Lord that gives us Salvation:

"For Him (alone) is prayer in Truth: any others that they call upon besides Him hear them no more than if they were to stretch forth their hands for water to reach their mouths but it reaches them not: for the prayer of those without Faith is nothing but (futile) wandering (in the mind)." (Quran 13:14)

The Holy Quran explains that works are to our benefit:

"O you whose hearts have been touched with the divine hand: When you intend to stand before God for performing your act of worship, then ablution becomes a duty. Wash your faces, your hands and the forearms up to the elbows, and with your wet hands wipe your heads, then wash your feet to the ankles....God does not intend to put you in difficulty but only to make you sound headed men of proper discipline and excellent mind, and to set you upon a course of purity of thought and action, for the actions of men are best interpreters of their thoughts, and He means to make all grace abound in you that you may hopefully actuate yourselves with the feeling of gratitude and gratefulness and lift Him your inward sight." (Quran 5:6)

The Holy Quran teaches us that Jesus came only to clarify the previous scripture, not to change it, and to promote the most important law, to worship our Creator:

"When Jesus came with clear proofs (of Allah's Sovereignty), he said: I have come unto you with wisdom, and to make plain some of that concerning which ye differ. So keep your duty to Allah, and obey me."

"For Allah, He is my Lord and your Lord: so worship ye Him: this is a Straight Way." (Quran 43:63-64)

(F.) TRINITY

Feeling Tempted?

Errancy; Christians claim that God needed to send Jesus to earth to know the temptations of the flesh in order to defeat it;

"Jesus returned from the Jordan full of the Holy Spirit and was led by the Spirit into the desert, where he was tempted by the Devil for forty days." (Luke 4:1-2)

"For what the law could not do, in that it was weak through the flesh, God sending his own Son in the likeness of sinful flesh, and for sin, condemned sin in the flesh" (Romans 8:3)

Excuse; None available.

Correction: Allah the Almighty clearly does not need to send anyone to learn about temptations.

Allah does not need to come down because He is already aware of everything that goes on everywhere and does not need to descend from the Heaven to see anything for He can already see it:

"It was We Who created man, and We know what dark suggestions his soul makes to him: for We are nearer to him than (his) jugular vein." (Quran 50:16)

The Holy One?

Christian Question; "We believe and know that you are the Holy One of God. (John 6:69) *Vs* "And Jesus said to him, "Why do you call me good? No one is good but God alone." (Mark 10:18)

Priest's Excuse; That is what it says but that is not what it means. Astoundingly, apologists reinterpret (Mark 10:18) to say; 'do you realize your calling me God'

Muslim Reply: The Bible scholars ignore the context yet the preceding passage debunks their distortion;

"a man ran up and knelt before him, and asked him, good teacher" (Mark 10:17)

Therefore, Jesus was being called a teacher, as were other men including Barnabas and Simeon (Acts 13:1)

In fact, according to Paul, a "teacher" is fourth in the chain of authority;

"And God hath set some in the church, first apostles, secondarily prophets, thirdly teachers, after that miracles, then gifts of healings, helps, governments, diversities of tongues." (1 Corinthians 12:28)

The first is God, second are the apostles (obviously Paul thinks highly of himself), and third in line of religiousness are the Prophets, and Fourth are the Teachers. Therefore, it is a far stretch for the Bible scholars to take the word "teacher" in (Mark 10:17) and make it jump to the head of the Spiritual line.

Thus, the man approaching Jesus had no objective of calling Jesus "divine"; instead, the man was commenting on Jesus being one who was a teacher. Jesus was a teacher and a messenger, guiding and teaching people the truth of their Lord.

At this point, Jesus refuted the man saying, "Only God is good", meaning; only God has all the knowledge, above all others in wisdom. We understand this meaning as it is repeated by Jesus in this passages;

"But of that day and hour no one knows, not even the angels in heaven, nor the Son, but only the Father." (Mark 13:32)

And

"So Jesus answered them, "My teaching is not mine, but His who sent me" (John 7:16)

The second reason we know the word "teacher" in (Mark 10:17) has no Divine significance is because throughout the entire Bible, God is never referred to with the noun: "Teacher".

In conclusion, for Christians to warp a passage where Jesus is clearly denying being the Holy One (and does not deny being a "teacher" – the fourth in line of religious stature-), is a disservice to humanity.

Quranic Answer: "Allah is He, than Whom there is no other god;- the Sovereign, the Holy One, the Source of Peace (and Perfection), the Guardian of Faith, the Preserver of Safety, the Exalted in Might, the Irresistible, the Supreme: Glory to Allah! (High is He) above the partners they attribute to Him." (Quran 59:23)

The Peace?

Christian Question; "God was pleased through him to reconcile to himself all things by making peace through his blood, shed on the cross." (Colossians 1:19, 20) *Vs* "Think not that I am come to send peace on earth: I came not to send peace, but a sword." (Matthew 10:34)

Priest's Excuse; That is what it says but that is not what it means; there is a distinction between the purpose and the result.

Muslim Reply: We still see that even if we only focus on the result (rather than the purpose to "send a sword to earth"); Jesus is noted within the Bible to have come and left us with commotion since his birth.

"He gave orders to kill all the boys in Bethlehem and its neighborhood who were two years old and younger-this was done in accordance with what he had learned from the visitors about the time when the star had appeared." (Matthew 2:16)

And after Jesus departed;

"Then some Jews came from Antioch and Iconium and won the crowd over. They stoned Paul and dragged him outside the city, thinking he was dead." (Acts 14:19)

We see that when Jesus came to the earth and when he departed from the earth, there was commotion as was the case with all Prophets. The farfetched claim that Jesus reconciled "all things" by "making peace through his blood" does not possess any validity. "All things" were and are not at peace as the Bible claims Jesus established.

Quranic Answer: The Holy Quran clarifies that Allah, unlike Jesus, is the source of Peace and can truly bring peace but that peace is conditional on the humans' freedom to choose peace. The Quran gives us multiple corrections in that 1) there was no unconditional blood sacrifice in the Quran and 2) Allah teaches us how to truly attain peace in the Quran:

"And remember Abraham said: "My Lord, make this a City of Peace, and feed its people with fruits,-such of them as believe in Allah and the Last Day." He answered: As for him who disbelieveth, I shall leave him in contentment for a while, then I shall compel him to the doom of Fire - a hapless journey's end!" (Quran 2:126)

Therefore, Allah answered the prayer of Prophet Abraham, but specified the conditions for peace.

"Wherewith Allah guideth him who seeks His good pleasure to ways of peace and safety, and leadeth them out of darkness, by His will, unto the light,- guideth them to a path that is straight." (Quran 5:16)

Peace is not granted unconditionally to everyone through a blood sacrifice as the Bible claims; instead, there are various realistic conditions to receive peace from the Giver of Peace:

"But if the enemy inclines towards peace, do thou (also) incline towards peace, and trust in Allah: for He is One that heareth and knoweth (all things)." (Quran 8:61)

Other than the conditions for peace on earth, the Quran clarifies that the ultimate place of Peace is in Heaven, where tranquility is truly conciliated:

"(This will be) their cry therein: "Glory to Thee, O Allah!" And "Peace" will be their greeting therein! And the close of their cry will be: "Praise be to Allah, the Cherisher and Sustainer of the worlds!" (Quran 10:10)

"But Allah doth call to the Home of Peace: He doth guide whom He pleaseth to a way that is straight." (Quran 10:25)

In conclusion, God teaches us that1) peace on earth is conditional and those who sincerely seek peace will receive peace; 3) the ultimate place of peace is Heaven. Finally, unlike Jesus, God in the Quran is the Source of Peace:

"Allah is He, than Whom there is no other god;- the Sovereign, the Holy One, the Source of Peace (and Perfection), the Guardian of Faith, the Preserver of Safety, the Exalted in Might, the Irresistible, the Supreme: Glory to Allah! (High is He) above the partners they attribute to Him. (Quran 59:23)

Trusted?

Christian Question; "Trust in God; trust also in me (John 14:1) *Vs* "(Jesus said) "Go to the festival yourselves. I am not going to this festival, for my time has not yet fully come." After saying this, he remained in Galilee; but after his brothers had gone to the festival, he went also, not openly, but in secret." (John 7:8-10)

Priest's Excuse; It was not a lie because Jesus did not go in the fashion the brothers wanted him to, they wanted Jesus to go openly, and Jesus went privately.

Muslim Reply: The issue is not whether Jesus was intending to go privately instead of out in the open, the subject is that Jesus claimed to have stated "I'm not going", and as soon as the brothers left, In the Bible, Jesus is depicted to have broken his word and went.

Quranic Answer: We see from the Quran we can consistently put our Trust in God "And put thy trust in Him Who lives and dies not; and celebrate his praise; and enough is He to be acquainted with the faults of His servants" (Quran 25:58)

The Protector?

Christian Question; The Bible alleges that those who are one with Jesus will be protected by Jesus "I am the gate: whoever enters through me will be kept safe." (John 10:9)

Besides the fact that according to the Bible, Jesus was not even able to protect himself (irrespective of repeated efforts) on the cross – we also witness that the self proclaimed number one apostle of Jesus; [Paul] was also not kept safe, despite the alleged promise of safety from Jesus;

"Then some Jews came from Antioch and Iconium and won the crowd over. They stoned Paul and dragged him outside the city, thinking he was dead." (Acts 14:19)

Therefore, Jesus did not have the sole power to be a protector for himself or those devoted to him.

Priest's Excuse; God wanted Jesus to die, which is why the prayers by Jesus to protect himself were not answered.

Muslim Reply: Here is where Christian apologists confuse the Bible even more. On the one hand, Christians claim Jesus is God, and as we have read, Jesus obviously wanted to be saved and protected from the cross.

Nevertheless, in order to explain the contradiction, Christians try to have it both ways by saying at that moment, Jesus was not God, and the Real God did not want Jesus saved.

The Christians try to have their cake (sacrifice) and eat it too (salvation). Christians claim that their trinity is One God. If so, how could their 'One God' want two different things at that same moment? Here we uncover the fallacy for we cannot have One God fighting Himself to live.

Quranic Answer: The Holy Quran corrects this multi-mistake in the Bible by stating:

“Allah is the Protector of those who have faith: from the depths of darkness He will lead them forth into light. Of those who reject faith the patrons are the evil ones: from light they will lead them forth into the depths of darkness. They will be companions of the fire, to dwell. (Quran 2:257)

“Muhammad was sitting under a tree when a pagan with a sword approached him to kill him, the pagan asked ‘who will protect you’, Muhammad replied “Allah”, at this moment, the pagan lunged forward at Prophet Muhammad and tripped on a stump and dropped the sword which Muhammad picked up and gave it back to the pagan and asked the pagan, “who would have protected you”, the pagan replied ‘no, one’, from that day on, the pagan became a Muslim and one of Prophet Muhammad’s closest companions. (Volume 5, Book 59, Number 460: Narrated Jabir bin ‘Abdullah)

Mighty and Powerful?

Christian Question; “Christ, who is the head over every power and authority” (Colossians 2:10) *Vs* “I can of Myself do nothing. As I hear, I judge; and My judgment is righteous, because I do not seek My own will but the will of the Father who sent Me.” (John 5:30)

Priest’s Excuse; You must understand the context of the verse.

Muslim Reply: This is a false claim because there are an abundant amount of chapters in the Bible that contain no context, for example; Proverbs. The verses are a number of independent statements that skip through different subjects. Other examples include the discrepancies between Samuel, Kings, and Chronicles which contain verses about people and numbers which invalidate the out of context argument.

The context clearly goes on about how Jesus is defunct without his Creator.

Quranic Answer: “Have they not traveled in the land and seen the nature of the consequence for those who were before them, and they were mightier than these in power? Allah is not such that aught in the heavens or in the earth escapeth Him. Lo! He is the Wise, the Mighty.” (Quran 35:44)

And

“To the People of Pharaoh, too, aforetime, came Warners (from Allah). The (people) rejected all Our Signs; Therefore We grasped them with the grasp of the Mighty, the Powerful.” (Quran 54:41-42)

The Omnipotent One?

Christian Question; "Christ died and returned to life so that he might be the Lord of both the living and the dead." (Romans 14:9) *Vs* "You heard me say, `I am going away and I am coming back to you.' If you loved me, you would be glad that I am going to the Father, for the Father is greater than I." (John 14:28)

Priest's Excuse; That is what it says but that is not what it means. The son is less than the Father in rank, but not in nature.

Muslim Reply: At least there is a partial confession from the Bible scholars that Jesus is less than God. In summary, as Jesus is less than his Creator in any fashion, form or function (as Jesus himself admits is both), then logically, Jesus is not equal to God. For example: one cannot have less work than their co-worker and also claim to have an equal amount. One can say they are doing the same work, but analytically one's work is less than the other. The president and vice president are not equal even though they act as one in the company.

Quranic Answer: "Surely those who guard (against evil) shall be in gardens and rivers, In an Assembly of Truth, in the Presence of a Sovereign Omnipotent." (Quran 54:54-55)

"He is the Omnipotent, (watching) from above over His worshippers, and He sets guardians over you. At length, when death approaches one of you, Our angels take his soul, and they never fail in their duty." (Quran 6:61)

The Forgiver?

Christian Question; In one Gospel, there is the claim; "The Son of Man has authority on earth to forgive sins." (Mark 2:10) While in the Gospel of Luke, Jesus proves he has no authority to forgive;

"And Jesus said Father forgive them for they know not what they do." (Luke 23:34)

This passage demonstrates that Jesus did not have the unconstrained power to forgive yet is making supplication to his Lord for forgiveness. Jesus also confirms his lack of power; "To sit at my right hand and at my left is not mine to grant, but it is for those for whom it has been prepared by my Father" (Matthew 20:23)

Quranic Answer: "Say: "If ye do love Allah, Follow me: Allah will love you and forgive you your sins: For Allah is Oft-Forgiving, Most Merciful." (Quran 3:31)

The Omniscient?

Christian Question; "Christ, in whom are hidden all the treasures of wisdom and knowledge." (Colossians 2:3) *Vs* Jesus unaware of where the body of Lazarus is; "And [Jesus] said, Where have ye laid him? They said unto him, Lord, come and see." (John 11:34) and "But of that day and hour no one knows, not even the angels in heaven, nor the Son, but only the Father." (Mark 13:32)

Priest's Excuse; Due to Jesus being in 'flesh-man form', he did not know everything.

Muslim Reply: Here we have another confession from the Bible scholars that Jesus was not equal to God, therefore discrediting trinity. In order to justify (Mark 13:32), they confirm the contradiction in (Colossians 2:3) that claims Jesus knows everything while Jesus himself acknowledged not knowing everything.

Quranic Answer: "Say: None in the heavens or on earth, except Allah, knows what is hidden: nor can they perceive when they shall be raised up (for Judgment)." (Quran 27:65)

And

"Say: "Allah knows best how long they stayed: with Him is (the knowledge of) the secrets of the heavens and the earth: how clearly He sees, how finely He hears (everything)! They have no protector other than Him; nor does He share His Command with any person whatsoever." (Quran 18:26)

The Most High?

Christian Question; "God exalted him to the highest place and gave him a name that is above every name." (Phil 2:9) *Vs* "(Now that he (Jesus) ascended, what is it but that he also descended first into the lower parts of the earth?" (Ephesians 4:9)

And

"For Christ also hath once suffered for sins, the just for the unjust, that he might bring us to God, being put to death in the flesh, but quickened by the Spirit: By which also he went and preached unto the spirits in prison; Which sometime were disobedient, when once the longsuffering of God waited in the days of Noah, while the ark was a preparing, wherein few, that is, eight souls were saved by water." (1 Peter 3:18 – 20)

Note; (1 Peter 3:18 – 20) is reiterated in the (Apostles' Creed) as "[Jesus] who was conceived of the Holy Spirit, born of the Virgin Mary, suffered under Pontius Pilate, was crucified, died, buried and descended into hell."

Priest's Excuse; 1st) Jesus went to Hell to try to save some of the doomed. 2nd) The doomed were angels in heaven that Jesus tried to save.

Muslim Reply: 1st) This confirms Jesus is not the highest because his abode was the lowest in the Bible. Allah is the Highest, Most Supreme. 2nd) To claim Jesus was trying to save angels to avoid the embarrassing Biblical claim that Jesus descended to Hell rather than Heaven, is an affront to the obvious Bible passages and creed that says otherwise. Selective reading will not grant escape from Jesus descending to Hell in the Bible.

First, the reason why the unsaved souls in (1 Peter 3:18 – 20) were not angels is because they were from "days of Noah, while the ark was being prepared". We know that angels were created before men (Job 38:4-7).

Second, we know Jesus was not rescuing unsaved angels in Heaven because according to the Bible; Heaven is a place for the righteous while the abode for the unsaved angels is "Hell" (Matthew 25:41).

In (2 Peter 2:4), the imprisoned angels are in "Tartarus", a Greek word used to describe a place 'Lower than Hell'. Therefore, in an effort to defend Jesus from being in Hell, they have exposed Jesus to be in "Tartarus", a place lower than Hell.

Note; Some Christians try to insinuate that the Holy Quran suggests that Jesus will go to Hell because those who worship idols and their idols will go to Hell (Quran 21:98). The Jesus in the Gospel is similar yet different from the Jesus in the Quran in that there is no ambiguity concerning the entity of Jesus. Jesus will not go to Hell, because Muslims do not worship Jesus and Jesus never asked to be worshipped. The idols referenced in the Holy Quran may be the crosses and statues sprawled across most Churches.

Quranic Answer: Without dispute, the Holy Quran confirms God is the Highest: "His Throne doth extend over the heavens and the earth, and He feeleth no fatigue in guarding and preserving them for He is the Most High, the Supreme (in glory)." (Quran 2:255)

The Appreciative?

Christian Question; "Behold, I am coming soon! My reward is with me and I will give to everyone according to what he has done." (Revelation 22:12) *Vs* "Many will say to me in that day, Lord, Lord, have we not prophesied in thy name? and in thy name have cast out devils? and in thy name done many wonderful works? And then will I profess unto them, I never knew you: depart from me, ye that work iniquity." (Matthew 7:22-23)

Priest's Excuse; None available.

Quranic Answer: "That is (the Bounty) whereof Allah gives Glad Tidings to His Servants who believe and do righteous deeds. Say: "No reward do I ask of you for this except the love of those near of kin." And if any one earns any good, We shall give him an increase of good in respect thereof: for Allah is Oft-Forgiving, Most Ready to appreciate (service)." (Quran 42:23)

"For He will pay them their wages, nay, He will give them (even) more out of His Bounty: for He is Oft-Forgiving, Most Ready to appreciate (service)." (Quran 35:30)

"If you set apart for Allah a goodly portion, He will double it to your (credit), and He will grant you Forgiveness: for Allah is most Ready to appreciate (service), Most Forbearing" (Quran 64:17)

Answers Prayers?

Christian Question; "You may ask me for anything in my name and I will do it. (John 14:14) *Vs* Jesus apparently praying to God to be saved from the cross according to the Trinitarians;

"about the ninth hour Jesus cried with a loud voice, saying, Eli, Eli, lama sabachthani? That is to say, My God, my God, why hast thou forsaken me?" (Matthew 27:46)

Priest's Excuse; God wanted Jesus to die, which is why the prayers of Jesus to be saved were not answered.

Muslim Reply: Here is where Christian apologists confuse the Bible even more. On the one hand, Christians claim Jesus is God, and as we have read, Jesus obviously wanted to be saved. However, in order to explain the contradiction, the Christians try to have it both ways by saying at that moment, Jesus was not God, and the Real God did not want Jesus saved. Christians claim that their trinity is One God, if so, how could their 'One God' want two different things at that same moment? Here we uncover their fallacy because you cannot have One God fighting Himself to live.

Quranic Answer: God in the Holy Quran differentiates between the good and bad beings in regards to answering prayers:

"And your Lord says: "Call on Me; I will answer your (Prayer): but those who are too arrogant to serve Me will surely find themselves in Hell - in humiliation!" (Quran 40:60)

The Last?

Christian Question; "I (Jesus) am the first and the last, the Beginning and the Ending." (Revelation 22:13) *Vs* "I have yet many things to say unto you, but ye cannot bear them now. Howbeit when he, the Spirit of truth, is come, he will guide you into all truth: for he shall not speak of himself; but whatsoever he shall hear, that shall he speak: and he will show you things to come." (John 16:12-13)

Note; (John 16:12-13) is considered as one of the many predictions of Prophet Muhammad (pbuh) and the Holy Quran.

Priest's Excuse; That is what it says but that is not what it means. This is a prediction about the Holy Spirit, not Muhammad.

Muslim Reply: First, Trinitarians claim that the Holy Spirit, God, and Jesus are all one entity while Jesus was obviously speaking of someone other than himself in (John 16:12-13). Jesus spoke about himself in (v12) "I have" then switches from personal pronouns "I" to "he", rather then maintaining a constant personal pronoun of "I". Jesus does not say; "I will come later to finish speaking".

Second, another reason why we know that the Holy Spirit and Jesus are not one in the same is because of (Matthew 12:31); "Wherefore I say unto you, all manner of sin and blasphemy shall be forgiven unto men: but the blasphemy against the Holy Ghost shall not be forgiven unto men."

Yet after the thief next to Jesus on the cross –mocked and reviled- Jesus (Mark 15:32), Jesus forgave one and said you will go to Heaven (Luke 23:43).

Third, Jesus admits that he has nothing else to say; Jesus states that everything his Creator wanted him to say was already said;

"for all things that I have heard of my Father I have made known unto you." (John 15:15)

Which confirms an individual other than Jesus will say more. For example; it would be a symptom of schizophrenia for someone to say; "I said everything I was told, and I will come to say more from me and I will glorify myself and I will say nothing of my own will other than what I was told by myself".

One has a free choice of following the Trinitarians' perplexity or believing that (John 16:12-13) was one of the many logical predictions of Prophet Muhammad (pbuh) within the Bible.

Quranic Answer: God in the Quran states:

"He is the First and the Last, the Evident and the Immanent: and He has full knowledge of all things." (Quran 57:3)

The Granter of Security?

Christian Question; "Satan has asked to sift you as wheat. But I have prayed for you, Simon that your faith may not fail." (Luke 22:31, 32) *Vs* "And he was in the wilderness forty days, tempted by Satan" (Mark 1:13, Matthew 4:1, Luke 4:2).

In addition, the Bible states that Jesus was tempted by the Devil in all aspects of his life;

"For we have not a high priest who is unable to sympathize with our weaknesses, but one who in every respect has been tempted as we are, yet without sin." (Hebrews 4:15)

Therefore, Jesus cannot protect us from Satan when Jesus himself is tempted by Satan.

Priest's Excuse; Due to Jesus being in the flesh form, he was susceptible to temptation.

Muslim Reply: Here the Trinitarians confess Jesus was tempted, thus contradicting themselves regarding the divinity of Christ because the Bible also says God cannot be tempted;

"Let no one say when he is tempted, "I am tempted by God"; for God cannot be tempted with evil and he himself tempts no one" (James 1:13)

In conclusion, the Trinitarians are repeatedly telling us that Jesus is God while in the process; they are creating even more contradictions within the Bible. Jesus, by the characterization of his temptation cannot protect us from Satan when he himself is claimed to be enticed.

Quranic Answer: Allah, the Holy One in the Quran is our only True Protector:

"Secret counsels are only (inspired) by the Devil, in order that he may cause grief to the Believers; but he cannot harm them in the least, except as Allah permits; and on Allah let the Believers put their trust." (Quran 58:10)

The Everlasting?

Christian Question; "Jesus Christ the same yesterday, and to day, and for ever." (Hebrews 13:8) *Vs* We see that Jesus the man ceased to exist;

"With a loud cry Jesus died." (Mark 15:37)

Priest's Excuse; Jesus had to die to fulfill scripture.

Muslim Reply: This confirms Jesus was not everlasting, which affirms that as a man, Jesus was not God.

Quranic Answer: The Holy Quran describes a True and Everlasting God:

"Allah! There is no god but He,-the Living, the Self-subsisting, Eternal. No slumber can seize Him nor sleep." (Quran 2:255)

Therefore, not only does God in the Quran not die, but God does not even sleep!

"Allah! There is no god but He,-the Living, the Self-Subsisting, Eternal." (Quran 3:2) "And put thy trust in Him Who lives and dies not; and celebrate his praise; and enough is He to be acquainted with the faults of His servants" (Quran 25:58)

Begets?

Christian Question; Christians claim that God sired Himself;

"God said to Jesus,' You are my son today I have begotten you" (Hebrews 5:5)

Priest's Excuse; Mistranslation.

Muslim Reply: While modern Christians admit their previous notions were based on inaccurate information, much damage has already been done in regards to knowing Jesus.

Quranic Answer: God is unlike any other as the Quran shows us:

"Say: He is Allah, The One; Allah, the Eternal Absolute; He does Not Beget, Nor is He Begotten, and there is None Like unto Him." (Quran 112:1)

<u>The Word?</u>

Christian Question; "In the beginning the Word already existed; the Word was with God, and the Word was God." (John 1:1)

"The Word became a human being and, full of grace and truth, lived among us. We saw his glory, the glory which he received as the Father's only Son." (John 1:14) *Vs* "Every good gift and every perfect present comes from heaven; it comes down from God, the Creator of the heavenly lights, who does not change or cause darkness by turning." (James 1:17)

Priest's Excuse; That is what it says but that is not what it means. This is speaking of God's essence, not changing into a man.

Muslim Reply: Bible scholars have confused a miracle into a creation of God.

"The Word" in context from the Bible delineates the method used by God to create life;

"And God (said), Let there (be) light: and there was light." (Genesis 1:3)

With a word, God created our planet's source of energy, the sun. The sun and the word of God became one; that does not mean we worship the sun, nor does it mean that the sun is God as ancient cultures believed.

We see again that God creates many living creatures besides Jesus with a "word";

"Then God commanded, "Let the water be filled with many kinds of living beings, and let the air be filled with birds." (Genesis 1:20)

Unlike the people of pharaoh, we do not worship figures. If we follow the logic of the Trinitarians, those created with the "word" are considered divine.

Therefore, we see in the framework of the Bible, that the word becoming flesh is a commonplace action and does not denote divinity.

Quranic Answer: The Holy Quran clarifies this point perfectly by stating: "She said: My Lord! when shall there be a son (born) to I me, and man has not touched me? He said: Even so, Allah creates what He pleases; when He has decreed a matter, He only says to it, (Be), and it is." (Quran 3:47)

“The similitude of Jesus before Allah is as that of Adam; He created him from dust, then said to him: “Be”. And he was.” (Quran 3:59)

Necessary Dissention?

Forsaken; Christians claim that God needed to send Jesus to earth to know the temptations of the flesh in order to defeat it;

“Jesus returned from the Jordan full of the Holy Spirit and was led by the Spirit into the desert, where he was tempted by the Devil for forty days.” (Luke 4:1-2)

“For what the law could not do, in that it was weak through the flesh, God sending his own Son in the likeness of sinful flesh, and for sin, condemned sin in the flesh” (Romans 8:3)

Excuse; None available.

Correction: Allah is already the Omniscient; God did not need to send anyone to learn about your temptations.

God's knowledge and love can reach us without Him coming down in human form, furthermore, why not love or care to understand the billions before and after Jesus was on earth.

Allah does not need to come down because He is already aware of everything that goes on everything and does not need to descend from the Heaven to see anything for He can already see it:

“It was We Who created man, and We know what dark suggestions his soul makes to him: for We are nearer to him than (his) jugular vein.” (Quran 50:16)

(G.) AFTERLIFE

All Sins Equal?

Christian Question; Christians ask if all sins are equal and if the sins also have an equal consequence.

"For whoever keeps the whole law but fails in one point has become guilty of all of it." (James 2:10) *Vs.* "Two men owed money to a certain moneylender. One owed him five hundred denari, and the other fifty. Neither of them had the money to pay him back, so he canceled the debts of both. Now which of them will love him more?" Simon replied, "I suppose the one who had the bigger debt canceled." "You have judged correctly," Jesus said. (Luke 7:41-43)

The "debt" refers to a person's sin against God. There are many references in both the Old and New Testament on how various sins will be punished differently, proving that not all sins are equal. Some sins push us further away from God than others.

Priest's Excuse; None available.

Quranic Answer: God in the Quran is a fair Judge who confronts us on a system of accountability, where every decimal of bad or good we do is taken into consideration for a verdict:

"On that Day will men proceed in companies sorted out, to be shown the deeds that they (had done). Then shall anyone who has done an atom's weight of good, see it! And anyone who has done an atom's weight of evil, shall see it. (Quran 99:6-8)

Equal Reward?

Christian Question; Jesus gives a parable of Heaven says that those who work harder for their reward will be equal to those who work less (Matthew 20:1-16) *Vs* "And, behold, I come quickly; and my reward is with me, to give every man according as his work" (Revelation 22:12)

Priest's Excuse; That is what it says but that is not what it means. Some people do not have the opportunity to work as hard as others do, that is why in (Matthew 20), both were rewarded equally.

Muslim Reply: The workers who only worked for one hour compared to those who worked for nine hours had the same opportunity to work as many hours as they would like but the one hour workers were not as inspired or motivated to find salvation as the ones who worked nine hours;

“For the kingdom of heaven is like unto a man that is an householder, which went out early in the morning to hire labourers into his vineyard.” (Matthew 20:1)

Here we see that the house owner went out “early in the morning” and found the workers who worked nine hours ready and willing to be saved. As the early bird catches the food, so are those who eagerly seek God‘s Mercy. As for the workers who only worked one hour;

“And about the eleventh hour he went out, and found others standing idle” (Matthew 20:6)

These one-hour workers did not bother to search for work until hours later, and they only worked because of necessity rather than voluntarily as the morning workers. Thus we see both workers had the same opportunity to wake up early, but the ones who reluctantly worked are assumed unfairly rewarded the same as those who readily worked.

Quranic Answer: The Quran uplifts the Bible in that Allah is the most Just and gives us accountability:

“Surely Allah does not do injustice to the weight of an atom, and if it is a good deed He multiplies it and gives from Himself a great reward.” (Quran 4:40)

Untouched Males?

Christian Question; In an affront to 99% of humans world wide, the Bible makes an incongruous declaration that only a certain race, and certain gender, and certain marital status will be in front of God; “The hundred and forty and four thousand, which were redeemed from the earth. These are they which were -not defiled with women-; for they are virgins.” (Revelation 14:3-4)

Priest’s Excuse; None available.

Quranic Answer: The Holy Quran corrects this limitation of those who have the opportunity to go to Heaven by bluntly stating that Heaven is open for all and any who strive for it: “If any do deeds of righteousness, - be they male or female - and have faith, they will enter Heaven, and not the least injustice will be done to them.” (Quran 4:124)

Furthermore, being with a woman in a marital relationship is actually a blessing, not a defilement: "Permitted to you, on the night of the fasts, is the approach to your wives. They are your garments and ye are their garments." (Quran 2:187)

Light in Hell?

Christian Question; Hell is a place of darkness (Matthew 8:12) *Vs* Hell is a place of light (Mark 9:48)

Priest's Excuse; That is what it says but that is not what it means. Fire means a place of destruction and darkness means a place of lost ones.

Muslim Reply: We know that when the Bible is speaking of fire, that it means literal fire because in another passage, a man in Hell says;

"…dip the tip of his finger in water, and cool my tongue; for I am tormented in this flame." (Luke 16:24)

Again, we know that this passage is speaking literally of a flaming fire from this quote; "These two were thrown alive into the lake of fire that burns with sulphur." (Revelation 19:20)

Quranic Answer: Hell is indeed a place full of flames, and the Quran clarifies that the darkness Jesus is referring to is the molten liquid poured on the evil doers:

"Yea, such! - then shall they taste it, - a boiling fluid, and a fluid dark, murky, intensely cold!-" (Quran 38:57)

Therefore, instead of Biblical apologists trying to change word meanings or trying to think metaphorically instead of using literal logic, the Quran explains that the liquid used is dark, like the crust and smoke from lava.

"(It is) the Fire of (the Wrath of) Allah kindled (to a blaze)," (Quran 104:6)

A kindling blaze is the location of hell and boiling and dark is the liquid will meet the evil doers in the location. Thus, it is literally detailed in the Holy Quran.

One More Chance?

Christian Question; The Bible claims that once a believer loses faith, he or she can never return to God;

"For how can those who abandon their faith be brought back to repent again? They were once in God's light; they tasted heaven's gift and received their share of the Holy Spirit; they knew from experience that God's word is good, and they had felt the powers of the coming age. And then they abandoned their faith! It is impossible to bring them back to repent again, because they are again crucifying the Son of God and exposing him to public shame." (Hebrews 6:4-6)

Priest's Excuse; Biblical theologians differ in their interpretation of these passages, some concede that salvation can be lost, others claim it is a mistranslation; 'fall away' should be 'drift way' indicating there is still hope.

Muslim Reply: Whether [fall away or drift away], it is still "impossible" for one (v4) to return. Therefore, those apologists offer false hope by ignoring the context.

Quranic Answer: The Holy Quran acknowledges that people do "fall" or "drift" away from their religion, yet the Quran does not abandon people's hopes as the Bible does, the Holy Quran explains that Allah gives us more than a single chance to repent and be saved:

"Those who believe, then reject faith, then believe (again) and (again) reject faith, and go on increasing in unbelief,- Allah will not forgive them nor guide them nor guide them on the way." (Quran 4:137)

In the Quran, those who drift away are given chance after chance. Unlike in the Bible, those who go astray from the straight path, even once, are not able to return back to God.

<u>Death in Hell?</u>

Christian Question; The Bible claims that the sinners will be destroyed;

"And death and hell were cast into the lake of fire. This is the second death." (Revelation 20:14, 2 Thessalonians 1:9) while in contradiction, the Bible says elsewhere's that the sinners will live a torturous life; "And in hell he lift up his eyes, being in torments, and seeth Abraham afar off, and Lazarus in his bosom. And he cried and said, Father Abraham, have mercy on me, and send Lazarus, that he may dip the tip of his finger in water, and cool my tongue; for I am tormented in this flame." (Luke 16: 23-24)

Priest's Excuse; That is what it says but that is not what it means. Death in (Revelation 20:14) is not a physical one but maybe a spiritual one like Adam experienced from the garden of Eden.

Muslim Reply: Because the Bible does not speak about skin regeneration as in the Quran, we have to logically and scientifically take the word 'death' literally. Any human body (being thrown and trapped in fire), dies in Hell, as the Bible conflictingly says.

Quranic Answer: The Holy Quran clarifies that our skin will be regenerated in Hell; hence, we will be kept conscience to feel the fire:

"Lo! Those who disbelieve Our revelations, We shall expose them to the Fire. As often as their skins are consumed We shall exchange them for fresh skins that they may taste the torment. Lo! Allah is ever Mighty, Wise." (Quran 4:56)

"He who will be flung to the great fire Wherein he will neither die nor live." (Quran 87:12-13)

<u>Feeling the Fire?</u>

Christian Question; Does burned skin feel? According to the Bible, the sinners will be tormented in Hell's fire;

"And in hell he lifts up his eyes, being in torments, and seeth Abraham afar off, and Lazarus in his bosom. And he cried and said, Father Abraham, have mercy on me, and send Lazarus, that he may dip the tip of his finger in water, and cool my tongue; for I am tormented in this flame." (Luke 16: 23-24)

"Depart from me, ye cursed, into everlasting fire, prepared for the devil and his angels" (Matthew 25:41)

Yet according to doctors, burned skin no longer has the ability to feel because of the damaged nerve endings. The skin becomes hard and even burns off our body like charcoaled piece of meat. Therefore, the notion that we will continue to feel pain in hell according to the Bible is unexplainable and scientifically incorrect.

Priest's Excuse; None available.

Quranic Answer: The noble Quran teaches the skin is regenerated:

"Lo! Those who disbelieve Our revelations, We shall expose them to the Fire. As often as their skins are consumed We shall exchange them for fresh skins that they may taste the torment. Lo! Allah is ever Mighty, Wise." (Quran 4:56)

Conclusion

In the manner of Moses leading Jews out of Egypt, the Quran has also parted a sea of questions in the Bible to lead humans to Heaven. We come to several conclusions at the end of this monumental exploration. We have found that what thousands of Bible teachers could not do for thousands of years, the Quran has produced in a precise and clear method.

Another finding from our research is that the Holy Quran brings an acceptable balance between the Jews and Christians. For Jews, Jesus is turned from a carpenter to a Messiah, for Christians, Jesus is turned from a God to a Prophet, and the balance is made so that both Jews and Christians can accept each other and have a shared and plausible belief in Jesus and his Creator.

For Jews, Salvation was made easier, for Christians, Salvation was made harder, again giving a level of balance that both sides can agree on and accept. In addition, a clearer explanation was made of the fate of earth and the Afterlife. In both Judaism and Christianity, the Rabbis and Priests are stripped of their powers to reinterpret scriptures that caused humans to deviate from the path of God.

The pinnacle of unity that the Quran brings between Jews and Christians is the fate of Jesus. Christ is not used as a scapegoat in the Quran; there was no need for Jesus to die to achieve salvation as in Christianity. The Quran explicitly says the Jews did not kill Jesus, which was the fuel for many crusades and even the Holocaust according to many historians.

In Adolph Hitler's autobiography *Mein Kampf*, it's repeatedly proclaimed he was doing the "Lord's work." At a Christmas celebration in 1926, Hitler stated; "Christ was the greatest early fighter in the battle against the world enemy, the Jews ... The work that Christ started but could not finish, I -- Adolph Hitler -- will conclude."

Much of the Nazi propaganda labeled Jews as "Christ killers", it is my sincere belief that if Hitler and many of the persecutors of Jews, believed that Jews did not kill Jesus as the Quran teaches, then millions of lives would have been saved. In fact, during many of the crusades and the Holocaust, Muslim nations, who saw Jews as fellow monotheists who did not kill Jesus, sheltered and protected Jews from the chasing crusaders. The Quran arbitrates between Jews and Christians to unite them as brotherly and sisterly Muslims.

Modern technology has and will increase the already fastest growing religion in the world simply because the internet and powerful search engines are allowing people to discover how Islam towers in truth above other religions in a magnitude unfathomed before.

The deeper we are able to look inside texts, pin pointing words and phrases for comparison, the more we are able to discover the Divine nature of the Quran. This is even more proof that in the days of Prophet Muhammad (pbuh), where computers were over a millennium away, it would have been impossible for a human to make the corrections because today it is taking extensive computer assisted researching just to realize that these corrections exist. For example, modern surgeons use endoscopes to search deep inside passages just as computers as used by authors to search deep inside passages, both discovering the works by God and detailed information unavailable to humans prior to these powerful searching tools.

We have also managed to dispel many myths by completing this massive manuscript. We have manifested how the Quran mends, rather than mimics the Bible. Furthermore, we have established that the Quran is not from Satan as some anti-Islamic preachers claim. In fact, by Islam re-confirming the validity of the laws in the Bible, the Quran actually exposes an attempt by Satan to lead people away from God. Satan from the start (with Adam and Eve), tried to get humans not to obey God, as Satan tricked humans with a brown tree and red apple, it was done again with a brown cross and red blood. Meaning most Christians have been led to assume that they are no longer responsible for obeying the laws of God, claiming the blood of Jesus on the crucifix atoned all their sins and made them closer to God. This is exactly the same type of manipulation Satan maneuvered on Adam and Eve; Satan told Adam and Eve if they accept the red apple on the brown tree, they too would become more God like. The sinister constant in both scenarios is; taking shortcuts that outcome in disobeying God. In the Quran, this salvation shortcut that people are tempted within the Gospel is removed, instead we are taught as in Judaism, that everyone is responsible for their own sins, thus keeping the laws as well as faith in God are both the keys to salvation, rather than just one or the other.

There are many more miracles in the Quran including scientific, mathematical, and literarily astonishments. Consequently, the Quran not only stands on its own, but also rescues the Bible. In closing, while there are over 100 valid answers, if the reader reluctantly accepts only one way the Qur'an answers Christians concerns about the Bible, then the reader must realize it is a blessing and not an attack on the Bible. The Quran helps the reader believe the stories in the Bible. Thus, Islam is the world's fastest growing religion simply because truth prevails. At the time of Prophet Muhammad (pbuh), the ratio of Muslims compared to Jews and Christians were; one Muslim for every million Jews and Christians. Today the ratio is, one Jew for every 100 Muslims, and the ratio gap between Muslims and Christians has dissipated down to 1 Muslim for every 2 Christians. According to "The Almanac Book of Facts", the population increased 137% within the past decade, Christianity increased 46%, while Islam increased 235%.

We invite the non-Muslim readers to accept Islam (submission to God) as taught in the Holy Quran. We leave you with a translation of an invitation letter to Islam from Prophet Muhammad (pbuh) to the former non-Muslim Kings of the Middle East:

"Praise be to Allah, the King, the All-Holy, the Peacemaker, the Keeper of Faith, the Watcher. He is Allah, there is no divinity but He, the Sovereign Lord, the Holy One, the All-peaceable, the Keeper of Faith, the Guardian, the Majestic, the Compeller, the All-sublime. Glorified be Allah from all that they associate with Him. And I testify that Jesus, son of Mary, is the spirit of Allah and His Word which He cast to Mary the Virgin, the good, the pure, so that she conceived Jesus. Allah created him from His Spirit and His Breath as He created Adam by His Hand and His Breath. I call you to Allah, the Unique, without partner, to His obedience, and to follow me and to believe in that which came to me, for I am the Messenger of Allah. Peace be upon all those who follow true guidance."

May God bless you with the hunger for knowledge and the ability to accept the truth once the knowledge has come to you.

We also invite the Muslims to fulfill your duties in inviting non-Muslims to Islam. In the same endeavor that this research has been made for the non-Muslims, we made this book equally for the Muslims. We pray that the Muslims have found this book confidence building and has given Muslims the optimism to invite non-Muslims.

Dozens of Bible Universities offer an increasingly popular degree in trying to solve Bible issues. Instead of these young men and women spending years of their lives to become apologists, we encourage you the reader, to invite these college students and even their professors to discover the simple and complete way the Quran answers all of these questions and more.
In my own public and private comparative religion debates with Jews and Christians, I have found this richly loaded compilation very useful and easily used as a topical encyclopedic [reply and answer] stockpile. Any one of the ways the Quran helps the Bible in this book are a point of dialog on the similarities and superiority of the Quran. The beginning and ending of the debate between you the Muslim and the non-Muslim are already mapped out for you here, to prepare you and give you the instrument to effectively show the Light and Love of God in the Quran to the non-Muslim. We are commanded over seventeen times in the Holy Quran specifically to invite the people of the Book (Jews and Christians), to the path of Allah.

For example:

CONCLUSION

"Say: O People of the Book! Come to an agreement between us and you: that we shall worship none but Allah, and that we shall ascribe no partner unto Him, and that none of us shall take others for lords beside Allah. And if they turn away, then say: Bear witness that we are they who have surrendered (unto Him)." (Quran 3:64)

Besides inviting Christians, we must increase our efforts 100% to invite the Jews. Muslims inviting Jews to Islam is very rare. God gave us the Quran to share with both the Jews and Christians. Prophet Muhammad (peace and blessings upon him) teaching us by example, himself invited Jews to Islam and also sent Muslims to convert Jews, and promised they will be greatly Blessed. In conclusion, our disobedience, pessimism and lack of confidence towards inviting Jews to Islam has resulted in Israel being the only non-Muslim country in the Middle East.

The Trinitarian Christian group "Jews for Jesus" has converted 300,000 Jews. The Jews endured the Crusades and Holocaust at the hands of the Christians, and Christianity teaches that the Laws of Moses are like rags to be done away with, yet nearly half a million Jews accepted Christianity just by the Christians asking them to. So fulfill your duty and simply ask non-Muslims to become Muslims and fulfill their duty to God as we're commanded to:

"Invite (all) to the Way of thy Lord with wisdom and beautiful preaching; and argue with them in ways that are best and most gracious: for thy Lord knoweth best, who have strayed from His Path, and who receive guidance." (Quran 16:125)

Bibliography

Abdullah, Yusuf Ali. *The Holy Qur'an, English Translation of the Meanings and Commentary*. Madinah, Saudi Arabia: King Fahd Holy Qur'an Printing Complex, 1991.

Abou Shabanah, Mirvet. *A Favourable Aspect of the Quran in Honouring the Woman*. Cairo, Egypt: The Supreme Council of Islamic Affairs, 1999.

Ahmed, Mansur and Saifullah, Muhammad and Ghoniem, Muhammad. *Refutation Of The Borrowing Theories Of The Qur'an. English.* http://www.islamicawareness.org/Quran/Sources/:Oct. 20, 2003.

Ajijola, AlHaj A.D. *The Myth of the Cross*. Lahore, Pakistan: Islamic Publications Limited, 1975.

Al Fandy, Muhammad Jamaluddin. *On Cosmic Verses in the Quran*. Cairo Egypt: Supreme Council for Islamic Affairs, 1994.

Ali, Maulana Muhammad. *History of the Prophets as Narrated in the Holy Quran Compared with the Bible*. Columbus, OH: Ahmadiyya Anjuman Isha'at Islam Lahore, Inc, 1996.

Archer, Gleason L. *New International Encyclopedia of Bible Difficulties*. Grand Rapids, Michigan: Zondervan, 1982.

Bucaille, Maurice. *The Bible, the Quran, and Science*. Indianapolis, IN: American Trust Publications, 1979.

Burr, William Henry. *Self-Contradictions of the Bible*. New York, NY: A. J. Davis and Company, 1860.

Clarke, Adam and Earle, Ralph H. *Adam Clarke's Commentary on the Bible*. Nashville, TN: World Bible Publishing, 1996.

Deedat, Ahmed. *Was Jesus Crucified?* Chicago, IL: Kazi Publications, 1992.

Dirks, Jerald F. *The Cross and The Crescent*. Beltsville, MD: Amana Publications, 2003.

Fatoohi, Louay and Al Dargazelli, Shetha. *History Testifies to the Infallibility of the Quran*. Kuala Lumpur: A.S. Noordeen, 2001.

Geiger, Abraham. *Judaism and Islam.* New York, NY: KTAV Publishing House, Inc., 1970.

Geisler, Norman and Howe, Thomas. *When Critics Ask.* Grand Rapids, MI: Baker Books, 1992.

Geisler, Norman and Saleeb, Abdul. *Answering Islam; The Crescent in Light of the Cross.* 2nd ed. Grand Rapids, MI: Baker Book House, 2002.

Geisler, Norman L. and Brooks, Ronald M. *When Skeptics Ask.* Wheaton, Ill: Victor Books, 1990.

Geisler, Norman L. and Mackenzie, Ralph E. *Roman Catholics and Evangelicals; Agreements and Differences.* Grand Rapids, MI: Baker Book House, 1995.

Geisler, Norman L. and Rhodes, Ron. *When Cultists Ask.* Grand Rapids, MI: Baker Book House, 1997.

Ghounem, Mohamed. *Who Is Our Savior: Allah or Jesus.* Cairo Egypt: M.G. Enterprise, 2000.

Haley, John W. *Alleged Discrepancies of the Bible.* Grand Rapids, MI: Baker Book House, 1996.

Henry, Matthew. *Matthew Henry's Commentary on the Whole Bible.* Peabody, MA : Hendrickson Publishers, Inc, 1991.

Ibn Abdullah, Misha'al. *What Did Jesus Really Say.* Ann Arbor, MI: IANA, 1996.

Jamieson, Robert and Fausset, A. R. and Brown, David. *Jamieson-Fausset-Brown Bible Commentary.* Peabody, MA: Hendrickson Publishers, Inc., 1997.

Kaiser, Walter C. and Davids, Peter H. *Hard Sayings of the Bible.* Downers Grove, IL: InterVarsity Press, 1992.

Katz, Jochen. *Jesus and the 99 Names.* English. http://answering-islam.org/Who/99names.html:October 21, 2003.

McKinsey, C. Dennis. *The Encyclopedia of Biblical Errancy.* Del Mar, CA: Promethean Books, 1995.

Nave, Orville J. *Nave's Topical Bible.* Peabody, MA: Hendrickson Publishers, 2002.

Neusner, Jacob and Sonn, Tamara. *Comparing Religions through Law: Judaism and Islam*. New York, NY: Routledge, 1999.

Pickthall, Marmaduke William, and Arafat Kamil Ashshi. *The Meaning of the Glorious Quran: Text and Explanatory Translation*. Beltsville, MD: Amana Publications, 1994.

Richards, Larry. *735 Baffling Bible Questions Answered*. Grand Rapids, MI: Fleming H. Revell, 1997.

Shakir, Mahomodali. *The Quran Translation*. Elmhurst, NY: Tahrike Tarsile Quran, 1986.

Smith, Ben J. *Differences; The Bible and the Koran*. Nashville, TN: Cumberland House Publishing, Inc., 2002.

Strong, James H. *Strong's Exhaustive Concordance*. Grand Rapids, MI: Baker Book House, 1989.

The Bible, King James Version. Oak Harbor, WA: Logos Research Systems, Inc., 1995.

The Good News Translation. Grand Rapids, MI: Zondervan, 2001.

Torrey, Charles Cutler. *The Jewish Foundation of Islam*. New York, NY: Jewish Institute of Religion Press, 1933.

Torrey, R. A. *Torrey's New Topical Textbook*. Murfreesboro, TN: Sword of the Lord Publishers, 2000.

Wells, Steve. *Skeptic's Annotated Bible*. English. http://www.skepticsannotatedbible.com/:Oct 14, 2003.

Index

Lightning Source UK Ltd.
Milton Keynes UK
15 October 2010

161337UK00001B/248/A

9 780972 851862